Wildfile

DON CONROY & CHRIS WILSON

MENTOR PRESS

MENTOR
PRESS

This Edition first published 1997 by

MENTOR PRESS
43 Furze Road,
Sandyford Industrial Estate,
Dublin 18.
Tel. (01) 295 2112/3   Fax. (01) 295 2114

ISBN: 0 947548 82 3

Cover Design: Design Image
Design: Kathryn McKinney
Editing and Layout by Mentor Press

Printed in Ireland by ColourBooks Ltd.

1 3 5 7 9 10 8 6 4 2

Other Titles by the Authors

The Authors

Don Conroy & Chris Wilson

Don Conroy is one of Ireland's most popular writers and has written many books for children and young adults. Well-known as an artist and wildlife enthusiast, Don is actively involved in conservation and environmental work. Young people will be familiar with Don's regular appearance on Den TV.

Chris Wilson is warden of Wexford Wildfowl Reserve. Birds and wildlife have always been of major interest to him, in fact more a love, a passion and a way of life. He is South East Radio's Wildlife consultant.

Dedicated to
Ann and Gay
Christina O'Brien, Richard Conroy, David Conroy, John McGuire,
Laura Daly, Anne-Marie Nolan, Henry Partridge, Kevin McCarthy
Family and Friends

Long-eared owl (Ceann cait)

Contents

There is nothing more sacred in life than what is most simple.
J. M. Synge

Introduction

Most of us don't have to travel too far to get out into the countryside. Maybe it's a wood, the seashore, open farmland with hedgerows, or out onto the mountains. Observing wildlife is like being in a magical world, a world that harbours an astonishing variety of creatures. Birds, mammals, insects, trees, plants, grasses, fungi, lichens and microscopic organisms all inter-link and rely on each other to live in harmony. This world to which we all belong, but which many of us have forgotten, or become distracted from, is essential for our well being and for our very life's natural rhythms to survive.

In this beautiful and mysterious world, a hare lies in the sweet smelling grasses in her form. Lapwings build their nests out in the open, but with eggs cleverly disguised to prevent detection. The skylark sings, suspended on invisible strings, high in the sky above the wildflower-filled meadow. In the blackthorn thickets badgers have their setts and foxes their dens. Otters play on the river banks, while midges dance overhead. A grey heron stands, like a sentinel, watching the slow-moving water, waiting to stab for its meal of fish or eels. Mute swans move gracefully upstream.

Insects drone and bees buzz over a variety of wild flowers, while noisy rooks call from their rookery. A kestrel hovers over a field, almost stationary, watching and waiting, ready to drop like a stone on a wood mouse or insect. Sparrowhawks fly swiftly along hedgerows, darting through a gap to surprise an unwary songster, while her young call from an old crow's nest with a hunger that never seems to be satisfied. An old stone wall holds the nest of a wren, while the ruined castle nearby provides the roost for a barn owl family. Cross spiders build elaborate webs to catch passing insects. Moonlight gives its signal for the night creatures to venture out. Bats help keep insect plagues at bay, colourful moths take flight, and a vixen screams her wild song.

Wildfile is full of facts and activities to help you become more aware of the wildlife around you, as well as practical tips to recognise some of these magical creatures. It will also give you some ideas on how to help and enjoy our environment in your own special way.

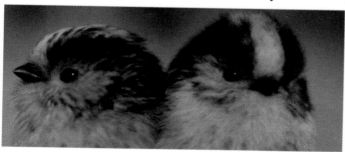

Long-tailed tits

I'm the eye of the Universe which sees itself and knows itself divine.
P. B. Shelley

Feeding Wild Birds

Dunnock

BIRD FEEDERS

Putting out bird feeders will attract birds quickly to your garden. These feeders can be hung near a window or from a bird table. By providing food and water you can help birds survive periods of severe winter and when food is scarce in early spring.

There are many ways in which you can help wild birds. One of the best and most direct ways is by feeding them. For your efforts you may be rewarded with all kinds of wonderful sights. Blue tits, great tits, coal tits, blackbirds, robins, song thrushes, starlings, house sparrows, greenfinches, dunnocks and chaffinches are all likely to come and feed from the food that you provide.

Leave water for birds as well, because birds get very thirsty and they love to bathe. Rarer visitors may appear in the garden during the winter months like siskins, blackcaps and even an occasional redwing.

Chaffinch

Should you feed birds all year round?

Many people wonder if it right to feed birds all year round. The answer is yes, but once you start you should continue. By leaving out food you are helping the adult birds keep their energy up. They will not feed the wrong food to their chicks.

FOOD SUITABLE FOR BIRDS
Most kitchen scraps
Oats, sunflower seeds, apples, pears
Cheese, bacon-rinds, suet, fat
Peanuts, breadcrumbs

(Wild-bird seed and peanuts may be purchased in most garden centres and supermarkets.)

Blackcap

AVOID
Salted peanuts.
Feeding white bread only.
Desiccated coconut.

REMEMBER
Water is essential on both hot and cold days.
Replace water regularly.
Never put additives into water for birds.

Robin (Spideog)

Best loved of birds, the robin is a favourite feature on most Christmas cards and many gardeners have the company of this bird as they dig the soil. It is noted for its tameness in towns and city gardens. The robin will even eat a meal-worm straight from the hand. In the countryside it tends to be a more shy and retiring bird. The male and female are alike with an orange-red face and breast with a pale grey/blue border and brown upper parts. Robins are very territorial and young birds have brown speckled plumage to prevent the parents from chasing them off while still very young.

Pair selection usually takes place in the early morning. During courtship the female chases the male until she is accepted by him. Once paired the male feeds her as part of the courtship ritual.

Robins nest in a variety of habitats and will readily avail of a nest box and even an old kettle in the hedge. They feed on insects, worms and berries and are regular visitors to bird tables in winter. The female moves away during winter months.

Where: Resident and migrant. Widespread. Likes an urban environment.

Food: Insects, worms, berries and fruit.

Nest: A cup made up of leaves, grasses and moss. Likes a hole or hollow in which to build the nest.

Eggs: Up to three broods of 3 to 9 white eggs, reddish spots and speckles.

Voice: The voice is fruity and clear with a change in the autumn/ winter song. The call is a clear sharp <u>tick</u>, <u>tick</u>.

Bird Tables

Here are instructions for making a traditional bird table. Ask an adult to help you.

Materials required

Wood

	Length
7.5cm x 7.5cm	1.8m. (for the post)
5cm x 2.5cm	4.6m
36cm x 36cm x 7mm	1 piece (for the base)
10cm x 7mm	3m
14mm dowel	30cm (for the perch)

Other

	Amount
4mm nails or 4mm screws	100g
Cup hooks	2 or more (for hanging peanut feeders)
Metal right angle brackets	4 (to screw the post and base)

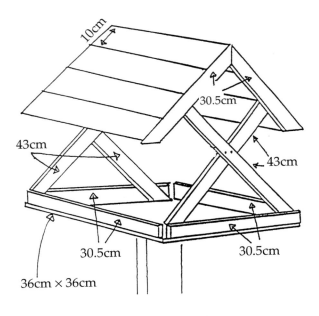

Assembly Steps

1. Attach the 30cm sides to the base.
2. Attach the joined 45cm (mortice) to the base.
3. Attach the roof latts.
4. Attach the perch between the cross members.

When the bird table is complete attach it to the post which, for convenience, should already be in ground.

REMINDER
Once you begin to feed birds, you must continue to do so right through the winter. Birds also need water, so replace it daily.

When finished, paint the entire bird table with an environmentally-friendly wood preservative if possible. Make sure the paint is dry before erecting your bird table.

A few nails or hooks along the side of the table will be useful for hanging nut bags.

Clean the table occasionally to prevent the possibility of disease. It is a good idea to periodically move the table to a different position so that bird droppings will not accumulate below it.

Keep the bird table away from walls, hedges and shrubs as cats and other predators may lie in wait and ambush unsuspecting birds.

How to MAKE A Bird Table

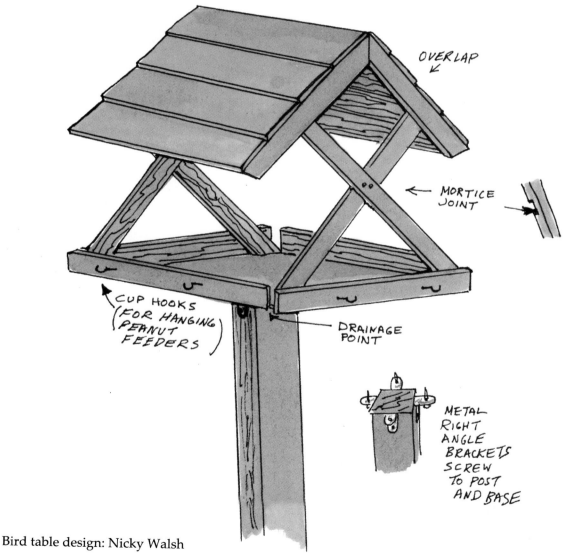

OVERLAP

MORTICE JOINT

CUP HOOKS (FOR HANGING PEANUT FEEDERS)

DRAINAGE POINT

METAL RIGHT ANGLE BRACKETS SCREW TO POST AND BASE

Bird table design: Nicky Walsh

Bird Nesting Boxes

Many bird species will use nesting boxes. Different bird species are attracted to a box depending on the size, position and entrance hole of the particular box constructed. Blue tits, coal tits and great tits will readily use a small-holed nest box, whereas birds like robins, flycatchers and wagtails prefer a larger opening.

For your garden or school grounds a standard bird box (shown on page 13) can be very useful.

> **MATERIALS NEEDED**
> A plank of wood 15cm wide and 1.5cm thick.

BIRD BOXES for TITS
The size of the hole varies with each species. A diameter of 2.5cm will suit the blue tit and the coal tit whereas 2.8cm is more suitable for the great tit. If you want to see house sparrows in your nest box the hole must be 3.2cm in diameter. (Now you can see just how important size is for different birds.)

BIRD BOXES for ROBINS, FLYCATCHERS AND WAGTAILS
For robins, flycatchers and wagtails make the same type of box as for the tits, but with the upper half of the front cut away.

Robin

Blue tit in nesting box

PLACING NEST BOXES
When placing the box on a wall or tree, remember to put a strip of wood behind the box. February, or even earlier, is a good time to put up your nest boxes.

> **AVOID**
> Placing the nest box in direct sunlight or where it may be exposed to heavy rain.

When do you clean out a Nest Box?
If and when a nest box is occupied make sure you clean it out in late autumn.

NEST BOXES for OTHER SPECIES
See page 46 on How to make a Barn Owl Box. Kestrels may also use a similar type of nest box to the barn owl. If you want to know about other species that may use nest boxes, contact Wexford Wildfowl Reserve for more information.

How to MAKE   A Bird Box

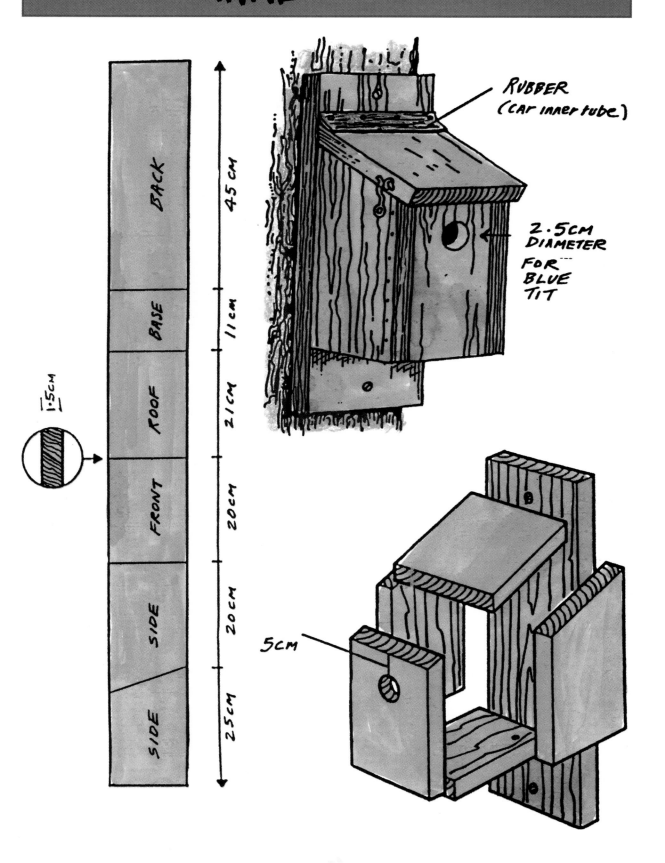

RUBBER
(car inner tube)

2.5CM
DIAMETER
FOR
BLUE
TIT

BACK

45 CM

BASE

11CM

ROOF

21CM

FRONT

20CM

SIDE

20CM

SIDE

25CM

1.5CM

5CM

Blue Tit (Meantán Gorm)

11cm

Blue tits are a common and widespread resident in Ireland. Blue tits literally put all their eggs in one basket, producing a single brood each year to coincide with the greatest number of caterpillars.

The blue tit has a bright blue cap and tail, bright blue wings, a greenish back and a yellow breast. Sexes are alike although the male does have a brighter blue cap. (See can you spot this difference.) Extremely acrobatic and active, blue tits can search out food at the tip of the thinnest twigs and are capable of hanging upside down on a branch. They are found in wooded areas and gardens, and they nest in holes in trees or walls in April and early May. The young are fed on caterpillars and remain in the nest for two to three weeks. Fledglings have greener caps and yellow faces. The tits remain together in groups for some time.

Where: Mainly a resident. Widespread.

Food: Insects, caterpillars, peanuts, bread, fat, cream from the top of milk.

Nest: A cup made up of moss, wool, leaves, hair. They love nest boxes.

Eggs: A single brood of 5 to 16 eggs, white with reddish brown speckles.

Voice: The blue tit has many calls. A high-pitched <u>tsee</u>, <u>tsee</u>, <u>tsee</u> is particularly common.

Grow Your Own Oak Tree

Try growing your own oak tree. This can be done by collecting acorns in the autumn.

1. Soak the acorns in warm water overnight. Take the cups off the acorns but do not try to remove the shell.

2. Place some stones at the base of a flower pot. This will help the water drain properly. Fill the pot full with compost or soil.

3. Place only one seed in each of the pots that you have prepared.

4. Cover the seed with a thin layer of soil and press it down to make it firm, then water the pots.

5. Place a plastic bag over the top of each pot and tie it with string or a rubber band. This will keep the inside moist without having to water.

6. Place the pot in a sunny place and wait for the seed to sprout. When it does, remove the plastic bag and water the seedling gently about twice a week, but do not soak as the seedling may rot.

7. If you can, place the pot outside during the summer time, then in the autumn plant the seedling in the ground.

8. Dig a hole deeper than the pot. Carefully remove the seedling and the soil from the pot, and place them in the hole. Fill the hole completely with soil and firm it down.

Remember to water the seedling regularly.

> You may try growing other trees in a similar way.

If you place an acorn on your windowsill, you protect the house from being struck by lightning.
Norwegian Legend

How to MAKE A Wildlife Pond

Having a small pond in a garden or in the school grounds can be a lovely addition to an area. Water is a magnet for a variety of wildlife, especially birds as they can come to drink and bathe.

You must plan your pond and its location very carefully. If you place a pond near trees it will soon fill with leaves. A sunny place is best.

If you want to put in fish, make sure there are different depths of water, as in warm weather fish can get too hot if the pond water is shallow. In summer the fish can dive deeper for cooler water and shade. It is the reverse in winter. The surface water may be too cold for them while the deeper water stays relatively warm.

CHOICE of LINING

A thick polythene or butyl sheet is ideal (but it must be flexible).

You can make any shape you like. Use good quality material as it lasts longer.

MAKING the POND

Mark the pond shape out with pegs and string. Dig a hole to required depths. Gradually sloping sides are best as they are easier to line, are better for planting and wildlife will prefer them. It is important to remove any sharp objects from the bottom and edges of the hole before you line it. You can use newspapers or old carpet to create a cushion underneath the lining. Sand or soil is probably better in the long run, but again make sure there are no sharp stones.

When this is completed spread the lining over the shaped hole. Leave at least a 30cm overlap all around and weigh down the edges with smooth stones. The turf you dug up earlier may be used to cover the overlapping liner. Any left-over soil can be used to make a rockery somewhere nearby. It is a good idea to cover the lining with sand or fine earth.

FILLING the POND

Fill the pond slowly. Do not trim the lining until all the water has settled and pulled the sides of the lining into its natural position. When the pond is full and has been allowed time to settle, trim and bury the edges of the lining properly. It is wise to fix the liner edges permanently with smooth large stones, suitable rocks or even paving stones.

Let the pond settle for at least two weeks. Then if you wish you can plant some water-loving plants in the pond and other suitable plants around the edge.

SUITABLE PLANTS FOR A POND
Water forget-me-nots, water violet, water plantain, starwort.

Water irises or reed mace can be planted in containers and then submerged.

A bucket of natural pond water will help to provide some microscopic life. Ask friends for plants or go to your local Garden Centre.

REMEMBER
Where possible always try to use native plants and shrubs. Don't remove plants, or for that matter, frog spawn from the wild.

Frogs in pond

Frogspawn

Damselfly

Flag iris

17

How to MAKE A Wildlife Garden

Most gardens and school grounds have grass covered lawns or playing areas. Try, if at all possible, to develop part of this area by leaving it un-mown. You will be surprised to see what flowers and grasses grow and flourish of there own accord.

DEVELOPING A WILDLIFE AREA

First design the shape you want by marking the area. Dig up the turf as it is better to start from bare ground. Then prepare the soil for sowing (this is best done in the autumn). Try to plant a variety of flowers which will grow from April to October. There are specialist seed suppliers, where you can purchase packets of wildflower seeds. Some even supply native plants in pots such as primroses, cowslips and edible herbs. It is a good idea to have your wildlife garden near a wall as it will provide shelter. You can also plant ivy, honeysuckle and creepers to create a valuable combination of nesting and feeding opportunities.

> **TIP**
> Some seeds such as primroses, cowslips and violets need frost to get at them before they germinate, while others like the pea family need a good soaking in the winter soil.

Ox-eye daisy

Fuscia

St. John's wort

Foxglove

Sunflowers

SHRUBS and SMALL TREES

Shrubs and trees can greatly enhance your wildlife garden. Use native plants where ever possible (particularly those that produce fruit and berries). Birds can eat lots of fruit and berries that we are unable to eat.

Native plants are more likely to survive in our weather conditions. Ask for advice from your local Garden Centre.

REMEMBER
Some berries are poisonous. Don't try to eat them if you do not know what they are. If in doubt leave them alone.

Blackberry and elderberry

Cotoneaster

The Truth about Ivy

Ivy (Eidhneán) is a very mis-understood plant. People assume, wrongly, that it is a parasite on other plants – mainly trees. Ivy has its own special rooting system and will not harm a healthy tree nor, for that matter, will it pull down a well-built wall. Ivy is evergreen and as it grows, it often spreads thickly over ground, rocks, trees and buildings. This thick growth is particularly useful as a protective cover. In truth, ivy is a haven for all sorts of wildlife species. For example, barn owls use ivy to roost and shelter in; wrens, robins, blackbirds and many other songbirds build their nests and raise their young in the secure and safe shelter provided by ivy. Since the ivy is a late flowering species the flowers and fruit provide important food to many insects and birds when other food is scarce. Ivy flowers are yellowish green in colour. The fruit is black and has three to five seeds in each berry. Legend has it that Ivy had magical powers. It was dedicated to Bacchus, the God of Wine. This was probably because it is supposed to prevent intoxication.

BEWARE
All parts of the Ivy plant are poisonous to humans.

Collecting Feathers

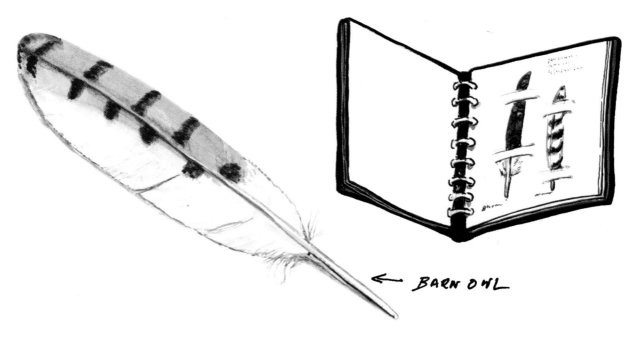

← BARN OWL

One of the many enjoyable pastimes available, is collecting. Different people collect different things: stamps, rocks, shells, books, call cards, train numbers. Almost anything can be the subject of a collection and people become passionate about many such hobbies.

One of the more fascinating and often overlooked hobbies is the collecting of bird feathers. Bird feathers come in a wide variety of shapes and sizes. Each feather has a special function. Some are soft, while others are firm, depending on whether they are for warmth or maybe for flight. Feathers can be found in almost any location and by collecting them you can become a 'Nature Detective'. A good way to keep feathers is by placing sheets in a ringed binder. The feathers are then fixed at the top and the bottom of the sheet. Another useful way to display a feather collection is using a photograph album, in which the feathers are placed under a clear sheet of plastic. Try and identify which species each of your feathers comes from and to what part of the bird's body the feather belongs. For example: primary and secondary feathers are flight feathers and come from the wing. Tail feathers can come from the centre or each side of the tail. Don't forget to note down where and when you found each feather.

Feather collecting is an in-expensive hobby that can provide valuable experience and pleasure. You will be surprised how quickly your collection grows!

We simply have to stop taking the earth for granted. It is, after all, the only home we've got.
Richard Branson

Drawing Nature

FEMALE LESS GLOSSY CAP AND LESS BLACK ON BELLY.

'GREAT TIT'
WEXFORD WILDFOWL RESERVE
JUNE 19ᵗ 96

People have been fascinated with observing and drawing wildlife for thousands of years. Cave paintings dating back to over 35,000 years in places like Altimira in Northern Spain are an example of how humans observed wildlife. It is not known fully why these first people of the earth painted their pictures. Some say it was to have magical powers over certain animals by drawing their image, others say it was simply to dress the walls of the caves. Whatever the reason, the tradition of drawing and painting wildlife continues to this day. You will see wonderful examples of a variety of natural history paintings in galleries, books, magazines etc.

You must teach the children that the land is sacred.
Chief Seattle

Making Wildlife Notes

Keeping a wildlife notebook/diary is very important. In our rapidly changing environment the notes we take today are not only interesting to us personally, but can be important, for comparison purposes, in future years. We all know that when we tell a story to someone, and then our story is re-told, many of the facts can change. This can be true of our observations of wildlife. There is no more important fact about an event than the original notes we took at the time.

When going out into the field, not only should you record the *Day, Date, Time* and *Place*, but also make some notes about the *Weather* and what other *Birds, Flowers, Insects* and *Mammals* you saw.

If you don't know the identity of a particular species, it is important to describe it in as much detail as possible. Make a note of exactly what it was doing, where it was, and any sounds it made. These small details will help you later, when using your books, to help you with identification. A drawing, no matter how brief and sketchy, can also help. The key to a positive identification, is the amount of details that you can note down in your Wildlife Diary. Quite often the bird or animal will only be in view for a short length of time, so those few moments that you are able to watch are very important.

At least when trying to identify plants they don't fly or run away and you can go back to the area on another day. With birds you would be surprised how many birdwatchers, with plenty of experience, have lost valuable seconds or minutes looking through a bird book to try and identify the species. Instead they should have kept an eye on the bird itself, making notes of the shape of the bill, what colour the legs were, had the bird one or two wing bars, did it have an eye stripe and so on.

19ᵗʰ SEPT. 11 05 AM WEXFORD COLD/DRY

BLACK ON HEAD

BILL THIN

ROBIN SIZE

GREY PLUMAGE

LEGS BLACK

BACK GARDEN SITTING ON SMALL BRANCH THEN WENT TO BIRD TABLE DID NOT STAY MORE THAN A FEW SECONDS

REMEMBER

Always be careful of size. In certain situations, birds can look particularly big or, for that matter, small. Size is best compared with something that is there for comparison, such as another bird that you can identify – Is it slightly bigger than a robin? Maybe not as big as a blackbird?

TIP

Use a pencil for your notes – it writes in the rain and is waterproof.

Don and Chris's Wildlife Diary

Apart from the fun of observing wildlife, your very own Wildlife Diary can be read several weeks after you made your observations.

We have made several notebooks over the years. Here is an example of a joint page from Don and Chris's Wildlife Diary.

Diary Book 3. Page 32/33

Day: Saturday 12th April 1997
Time: 8.30am to 2pm
Visited: Wexford Harbour, North Slob, Raven Nature Reserve
Weather: Cloud: $^2/_8$
Wind: South-east Force 3
Sunshine: Bright
Rain: Nil
Visibility: Excellent
Temperature: 15.5°C

REMARKS

A beautiful spring morning. We (Don and Chris) first checked the hides at the Reserve, then looked over the Slob and finished off walking through the Raven — listening, watching, smelling and enjoying a beautiful spring morning.

ANIMALS

Rabbit, Hare, Badger, Fox, Pigmy Shrew.

COMMENTS

Noted our first young Rabbit playing near a burrow. Four Hares seen on the Slob. Tracks of a Badger noted in some soft mud below the pen. A Fox heard calling at first light. A Pigmy Shrew heard at 11.30am.

BIRDS

Little Egret (1), Great Crested Grebe (6), Little Grebe, Greenland White-fronted Goose, Pink-footed Goose (3), Canada Goose (2), Mallard, Teal, Pochard, Tufted Duck, Shelduck, Ruddy Shelduck (probably an escape), Red-breasted Merganser (1), Kestrel, Sparrowhawk (female), Peregrine (male), Marsh Harrier (Female), Water Rail, Moorhen, Coot, Pheasant,

32

Oystercatcher, Ringed Plover, Golden Plover (over 500), Lapwing (4 pairs), Grey Plover, Knot, Dunlin, Sanderling, Ruff (3), Curlew, Whimbrel (7), Black-tailed Godwit, Bar-tailed Godwit, Redshank, Spotted Redshank (6), Greenshank, Common Sandpiper (1), Woodcock (1), Snipe (one drumming), Black-headed Gull, Great Black-backed Gull, Sandwich Tern (2), Little Tern (1), Black Guillemot, Wood Pigeon, Stock Dove, Feral Pigeon, Collared Dove, Cuckoo (2), Long-eared Owl, Kingfisher, Skylark, Meadow Pipit, Sand Martin, Swallow, House Martin, Pied Wagtail, Grey Wagtail, Dunnock, Robin, Stonechat, Wheatear, Blackbird, Song Thrush, Mistle Thrush, Blackcap, Chiffchaff, Willow Warbler, Goldcrest, Blue Tit, Great Tit, Coal Tit, Long-tailed Tit, Treecreeper, Starling, Magpie, Jackdaw, Raven, Rook, Tree Sparrow, House Sparrow, Chaffinch, Brambling, Greenfinch, Goldfinch, Bullfinch, Linnet, Crossbill, Yellowhammer, Reed Bunting.

COMMENTS

91 species – a good tally: Of note - Lots of Greenland White-fronted Geese present, counted 493 in Bullock field. A flock of 88 noted flying north-west away from the Slob at 8.50am – are they going home to Greenland? Mallard – two broods seen, one with 6 young one with 9 young. Peregrine – stooped at a Golden Plover but missed, I wonder whether they will try and breed in Wexford again. The Spotted Redshank were very smart in summer plumage. Woodcock and Snipe on same day Wow! Black Guillemot – must be from Rosslare. Long-eared Owl – beautiful. Plenty of migrants around. Cuckoo, Chiffchaff, and Willow Warbler singing. The Skylarks are everywhere – magic. Crossbill, only our second singing record here. Tree Sparrows are very busy nest building. Brambling is late.

BUTTERFLIES

2 Orange Tips, 4 Green-veined Whites, Small Tortoiseshell, Peacock and an early Painted Lady. Spring is in the air. Lots of midges dancing along the Raven Wood road.

PLANTS

The wild garlic is out and there are plenty of daffodils about; What a beautiful day. Lovely to see so many trees in leaf; the hazel catkins are particularly fine this year. Violets are just beautiful.

33

reed beds, hedgerows, woodlands, forests, mountains, cities, parklands, gardens, orchards and many more.

Each species finds its own niche in these varied landscapes. Some are restricted to a few more specialised areas. Usually the most successful species are the ones that are least specialised (starlings and brown rats are a good example).

Estuary

Almost everywhere in Ireland has been affected by human influences. This has not always been a bad thing for our flora and fauna. Wildlife has made good use of these man-made creations – pastures, meadows, canals and buildings, plantations, reservoirs, to name but a few. For a small island Ireland can boast a wide variety of habitats – sea, sea shallows, coasts, islands, sand-stone and rocky shore, dunes, machair, cliffs, estuaries, rivers, lakes, callows, bogs, turloughs,

Mountainside

Reed beds

Coastal area

Woodland

When you know what to look for and where to look, an exciting world will open up for you. Whether you are going on holidays, visiting relations in the city or countryside, or simply looking out of the kitchen window into a garden, there is always something to see, discover and enjoy. Habitats can be big or small, outdoors or indoors – in fact everywhere you look, there is a type of habitat.

Farmland

Coastal island

Gannets

The great ecosystems are like complex tapestries – a million complicated threads, interwoven, make up the whole picture.

Gerald Durrell

Red Deer (Fia Rua)

The red deer is the largest of the three species of deer found in Ireland. Red deer are native to Ireland and are found mainly in Counties Kerry, Donegal and Wicklow. Kerry possibly has the only truly native stock of red deer as the others were introduced from Scotland in the 19th century. The stag (male) has multi-pointed antlers which he sheds in late February or March. A new pair begins to grow immediately. A royal stag is one with antlers that have twelve points. The red deer's coat is reddish brown with a cream coloured rump. The winter coat is darker and the hair is longer. Red deer prefer the margins of large forests, although they have adapted to more exposed conditions of mountains and moorland.

During the winter they tend to live in lower areas. They feed mainly on grasses and heather. The mating season takes place during September and October and is known as the 'rut'. Calves are born to hinds (females) in early June.

If you live near a forest where there are deer, look out for their lovely antlers shed in winter.

Where:	Mountain regions, forests
Food:	Herbivore. Grasses, twigs, buds, bark, fruit and mushrooms.
Breeding:	Impressive calls of the stags indicate mating season (rut). Young are born eight months later. Fawns have spotted coats and are well-hidden in long grasses.

Collecting Animal Signs

HOW TO MAKE A FOOTPRINT CAST

1. Simply get a plastic container (square or round in shape). Cut out the base so that only the sides are left.
2. Place the frame over the footprint being collected, and press into the soil. Try not to damage the actual footprint.
3. Mix Plaster of Paris powder (which you can get in most hardware shops) with clean water in a plastic bucket until it is thick and ready to pour.
4. Fill the mould carefully to the rim with the Plaster of Paris. Let it harden. It will not take long.
5. Remove the frame carefully and you have a beautiful cast.
   Over time you can make a fascinating collection of animal and bird tracks.

STAG ANTLERS

These can be found in late February or March

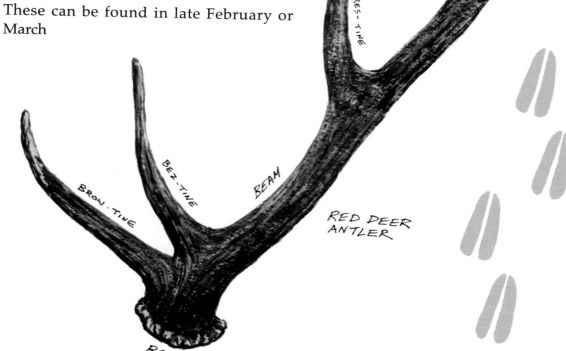

CROWN

TRES-TINE

BEZ-TINE

BROW-TINE

BEAM

RED DEER ANTLER

BASE

All of us who share this world have to live in harmony with nature, not in conflict with her.

David Shephard

Red Fox (Sionnach)

66cm long, tail another 38cm

The red fox is common throughout Ireland. Easily identified, the fox is a very adaptable creature and is traditionally found in woodlands. However, foxes are now common on farmland, boglands, mountain areas and have adapted successfully to urban life.

The fox's most distinctive features are its narrow muzzle, large ears and long bushy tail with a white tip. The coat is a reddish brown with light under-parts. Foxes are normally solitary and are most often seen at dusk. Young males, without territories, tend to roam widely. The vixen (female) is smaller than the dog (male). Although carnivorous, foxes will also eat insects, worms and fruit. Urban foxes will raid dustbins.

Mating begins in late December and January. The vixen gives out a powerful love call attracting dog foxes in the area. The young are usually born in February to mid-March in a dug-out burrow called a den.

Where: Widespread. Even found in towns and cities (where it has been noted that their legs are getting longer to help in jumping over walls and getting into dustbins: a new sub-species actually happening before our very eyes).

Home: A den. Sometimes an old rabbit burrow or part of a badger's sett is used.

Food: Carnivore. Varied diet of rabbit, small mammals, birds, insects, worms, berries and discarded food.

Breeding: Mating takes place in December and January. Litter normally four to five cubs.

There may be a number of dens in a territory and the mother may move the cubs to different locations for safety. The young are independent by autumn and fully mature a year later. Foxes can be very vocal at night, the males giving a high pitched bark whilst the vixen can produce an ear-piercing scream.

The fox is one of the most persecuted creatures of our countryside – it is shot, snared, poisoned, chased and hunted. Loved or loathed, Reynard is a survivor who brings his own special magic to the countryside.

Badger (Broc)

Badgers are common throughout the country and are essentially nocturnal. They are most often seen as they cross the road at night. They are instantly recognisable by their white face with its vertical black stripes. Their coat consists of a mixture of black and white hairs. Shallow scrape marks in the ground in woods can often indicate where badgers have been foraging.

Badgers live in groups in their den (or sett) which normally has between three and ten entrances. The sett contains chambers with bedding of straw, bracken, grass and leaves. This is replaced periodically, with fresh material. The badger is a member of the stoat, otter and mink family.

If badgers are threatened, they are able to puff themselves up to look bigger than they really are and they can move at a surprisingly rapid speed.

Where:	Widespread in woodland, hedgerows and copses.
Home:	Sett. A system of tunnels with play and sleeping areas. (They are very clean animals, even having special latrine (toilet) areas.)
Food:	Omnivore. Eats small mammals, birds, eggs, and vegetable food. Earthworms are a favourite part of their diet. They will raid bees' nests for the honey.
Breeding:	Mating is during February and March. Young are born the following year. The litter is usually three cubs.

Wexford Slobs

The Wexford Slobs are a natural haven for birds and other wildlife. Situated in the south-east of Ireland, the location makes this one of the warmer parts of the country, and therefore enticing to birds that are looking for milder wintering areas to feed and rest. Waders and wildfowl are particularly attracted to the area where the flat landscape creates a safe place to feed, roost and breed. In total 248 species of birds have been recorded to date, but it is the sheer quantity of birds in winter that makes this magical avian paradise so famous. Literally thousands of ducks, geese, and waders can be observed and enjoyed by all from October to April.

During the spring and autumn the slobs and harbour are also of international importance for waders and wildfowl. They make good use of the food-rich mud areas to feed on while on migration. The large shallow harbour beside the sloblands with its sand and mud banks is a magnet to birds arriving after long journeys from abroad.

The North Slob is immensely attractive to a host of wildfowl and waders and is internationally famous for its wintering flock of 10,000 Greenland white-fronted geese – Europe's rarest goose (a third of the world's population), and the wintering flocks of brent geese, Bewick's swans and wigeon.

The Pumphouse

Greenland white-fronted geese

Mammals recorded locally include badger, otter, stoat, mink, fox, wood mouse, and house mouse, red squirrel and bats (pipistrelle, long-eared, Daubenton's, and Leisler's). The Reserve lands and the North Slob, which are open grazed farmland, are particularly attractive to the Irish hare which is a protected species throughout the area. Grey seals and the occasional common seal are seen in Wexford harbour and there have been rare sightings and strandings of four whale species, two dolphin species and common porpoise.

Over 500 species of plant have been recorded in the locality with specialities including bristly ox-tongue (a thistle species), sharp rush, three-cornered leek, Borrer's saltmarsh-grass, great water dock, bee orchid, pyramidal orchid, three species of marsh orchid and a surprising number of other interesting plants.

The invertebrate life on the North Slob is also particularly attractive, with a large number of species occupying a wide variety of different habitats. Butterfly species recorded to date number 23, with specialities including common, holly and small blues, silver-washed and dark-green fritillaries, wood white, greyling and gatekeepers. Migrants such as red admiral, painted lady and even the occasional clouded yellow are recorded. Some of the more spectacular moths include the emperor moth, poplar hawk-moth, large and small elephant hawk-moths, eyed hawk-moth and even the beautiful looking humming-bird hawk-moth.

The Reserve was acquired primarily for the purpose of feeding and protecting the Greenland white-fronted geese during the winter months.

Visitors can enter the Reserve collection area, where the tame birds greet them in friendly surroundings. There is a modern visitor centre with displays about the slobs, its history and its birds. Visitor can climb the stairs, up to the centrally heated observation tower where superb views overlooking the North Slob give great views of the birds.

OPENING HOURS:

Summer: 16th April to 30th September
0900-1800 every day.

Winter: 1st October to 15th April
1000-1700 every day.

This amazing spectacle of these birds of the cold wind. just has to be experienced on the North Slob by the young and not so young. every winter.

Chris Wilson

35

Bull Island 'Visitors' Centre

One of the most exciting places to see birds and other wildlife is the Bull Island in Dublin. A low-lying sandy island in the northern part of Dublin Bay, this inter-tidal lagoon lies between the island and the main Clontarf-Sutton Road. The sand dunes and salt marshes contain a wide variety of wild plants and invertebrate animals, making this area a place of international importance. In winter over 40,000 wildfowl and wading birds arrive from their arctic breeding grounds to spend the winter months feeding on the rich plant and animal life in the mud flats.

BIRDS TO SEE on the BULL ISLAND
Some of the birds that you are likely to see, especially during the winter months, are: brent geese, wigeon, teal, shelduck, grey plover, lapwing, curlew, redshank, dunlin and bar-tailed godwit. Others, like kestrel, merlin, peregrine falcon and short-eared owl, are also known to visit. Kestrels, of course, can be present all the year round and have bred there successfully for a number of years. This is thanks to children from a nearby school putting up a nest box in which the kestrels could breed.

MAMMALS TO SEE on the BULL ISLAND
Mammals seen on the Bull Island include hare, rabbit, red fox, wood mouse, house mouse, pygmy shrew. A number of different bat species, including pipistrelle and long-eared, have also been seen. Out to sea you may spot common seals and grey seals.

WILDFLOWERS, BUTTERFLIES and INSECTS
There is a wonderful variety of wild flowers which includes sand-dune violet, bird's-foot trefoil, sea spurge, catsear, field speedwell and yellow rattle.

Saltmarsh

Five species of orchid have been recorded including bee and marsh heliborine. Butterflies, which can be seen on the wing through spring, summer and autumn include common blue, small copper, red admiral, painted lady, small tortoiseshell, three species of white and a number of other species. To date 420 species of insect and spider have been recorded at Bull Island.

A PLACE TO VISIT

This wonderful area is a magnet for the human species. Joggers, walkers, golfers, 'birders', painters, photographers, swimmers and picnickers all flock to the area. The people of Dublin are very proud of the Bull Island and with good reason. Do, if you can, pay a visit – and remember it is free!

Dunes

Hare

Don and Chris's Favourite Wildlife Places

INCLUDE THE FOLLOWING:
- Aillwee Caves, Co. Clare — Geology
- The Burren, Co. Clare — Geology, Plants, Insects, Birds, Mammals
- The Burren National Park, Co. Clare — Geology, Plants, Insects, Birds, Mammals
- Black Head, Co. Clare — Plants, Birds
- The Cliffs of Moher, Co. Clare — Seabirds
- Ballycotton, Co. Cork — Birds
- Cape Clear Island, Co. Cork — Birds, Plants, Cetaceans (Whales)
- Clonakilty, Co. Cork — Birds
- Cobh, Co. Cork — Birds, Moths
- Glenveigh National Park, Co. Donegal — Birds, Plants, Mammals
- Killybegs, Co. Donegal — Birds
- Malin Head, Co. Donegal — Geology, Birds
- Sheskinmore, Co. Donegal — Birds, Plants
- The Bull Island, Co. Dublin — Birds, Plants
- Church Island, Skerries, Co. Dublin — Birds
- Howth Head, Co. Dublin — Birds
- Lambay Island, Co. Dublin — Birds
- Rockabill, Co. Dublin — Birds
- The Irish Seal Sanctuary, Garristown, Co. Dublin — Seals in care
- Castle Espie, Comber, Co. Down — Birds
- Strangford Lough, Co. Down — Birds
- Aran Islands, Co. Galway — Geology, Birds
- Carraroe, Co. Galway — Birds, Plants
- Castletown River Turlough, Carron, Co. Clare — Plants, Insects, Birds, Rare Habitat.
- Connemara National Park, Co. Galway — Geology, Plants, Birds
- Oranmore, Co. Galway — Plants
- Portumna, Co. Galway — Plants, Birds
- Renvyle, Co. Galway — Plants, Birds
- Twelve Bens, Co. Galway — Geology, Plants, Birds
- Mount Brandon, Co. Kerry — Geology, Plants, Birds
- Castlegregory, Co. Kerry — Natterjack Toads
- Cloghane, Co. Kerry — Birds, Plants
- Dingle, Co. Kerry — Geology, Mammals, Birds
- Dunquin, Co. Kerry — Geology, Plants, Birds
- Killarney National Park, Co. Kerry — Plants, Mammals, Birds
- Puffin Island, Co. Kerry — Birds
- Skellig Michael, Co. Kerry — Geology, Birds
- Valentia Island, Co. Kerry — Birds, Plants
- Donadea Woods, Co. Kildare — Plants, Birds
- Inishbofin, Co. Mayo — Birds, Plants
- Banagher, Co. Offaly — Birds, Plants
- Clara Bog, Co. Offaly — Plants, Invertebrates, Birds
- Little Brosna, Co. Offaly — Birds, Plants
- Ben Bulben, Co. Sligo — Plants
- Ballagh, Co. Tipperary — Birds, Plants
- Cabragh Wetlands, Thurles, Co. Tipperary — Birds
- Cahir, Co. Tipperary — Birds, Mammals
- Cappamurra Cutover Bog, Co. Tipperary — Plants, Invertebrates, Birds
- Carhue, Co. Tipperary — Birds
- Cashel, Co. Tipperary — Geology
- Church Island, Lough Derg, Co. Tipperary — Birds
- Comeragh Mountains, Co. Tipperary — Plants, Birds
- Galtee Mountains, Co. Tipperary — Plants, Birds
- Goat Island, Lough Derg, Co. Tipperary — Birds
- Gortdrum, Co. Tipperary — Birds
- Killough Quarry, Co. Tipperary — Plants, Invertebrates, Birds
- Luska, Nr. Coolbaun, Co. Tipperary — Plants, Invertebrates, Birds
- Mitchelstown Caves, Co. Tipperary — Geology, Invertebrates
- Broad Lough, Co. Wicklow — Birds, Plants
- Glen of the Downs, Co. Wicklow — Plants, Birds
- Kilcoole, Co. Wicklow — Birds
- Wicklow Mountain National Park, Co. Wicklow — Plants, Birds, Mammals, Invertebrates
- Eden Vale, Co. Wexford — Plants, Birds
- Great Saltee, Co. Wexford — Birds
- Hopeland, Co. Wexford — Birds
- Our Lady's Island Lake, Co. Wexford — Birds
- The North Slob, Co. Wexford — Birds, Plants, Invertebrates, Mammals
- Raven Nature Reserve, Co. Wexford — Birds, Plants, Invertebrates, Mammals
- Rosslare Back Strand, Co. Wexford — Birds, Plants, Invertebrates
- Tacumshin Lake, Co. Wexford — Birds
- Wexford Wildfowl Reserve, Co. Wexford — Birds, Plants, Invertebrates, Mammals

FAVOURITE RIVERS

Blackwater, Dargle, Liffey, Multeen, Oranmore, Shannon, Slaney, Sow, Suir. Rivers are particularly attractive to many forms of wildlife including invertebrates, birds and mammals.

How to DRAW An Oystercatcher

Simply start with a soft pencil. HB or 2B are useful drawing pencils.

FIG 1

Start with these egg shapes. Indicate the bill, the eyes, the legs and the tail.

FIG 2

Connect up the egg shapes as shown.

FIG 3

Leave details to the end. This finished oystercatcher was painted over with a brush and ink. You can use a felt-tip marker or something similar. Rub out any unnecessary lines.

Don't worry about making mistakes. The Chinese, who are wonderful artists, have a saying: *You cannot call yourself an artist until you make 1000 mistakes.*

The reason these wise people say this is that when you are drawing you learn from each mistake. After all, there is no one correct way to draw.

Corncrake (Traonach)

The story of the Corncrake is well known as this species now has the sad and unfortunate distinction of being Ireland's only bird, at present, in danger of global extinction. Breeding commonly during the last century, the decline was first noted in eastern Ireland at the turn of the century. For many country people, born in the 1950s and before, the sound of the corncrake has actually become a nostalgic memory.

The corncrake is a summer visitor to Ireland arriving from April onwards. They winter in Africa. The male, who is the first to arrive, sets up his territory and starts his craking call. The corncrake is known for being a skulking and elusive bird. They can vanish, even in the thinnest of cover. Although appearing to have a weak fluttering flight, do remember, corncrakes are strong enough to fly to Africa. If lucky enough to see a corncrake, people are surprised to find that they are only about the size of a song thrush and are remarkably narrow birds – designed to move through thick grasses and vegetation. Currently they are confined to a few areas of rough grassland, hay meadow and callow land in the west of Ireland, a few offshore islands and in the Shannon Callows. Over the past two years the corncrake has made a slight recovery. This is due to the co-operation of farmers, the Birdwatch Ireland team and the National Parks and Wildlife Service.

Where: Callows, meadows, hay fields and islands.
Nest: Hidden in dense grass.
Eggs: 8 to 12, creamy with brown blotches.
Food: Mainly insects and worms. Will eat some seeds.
Voice: Distinctive repeated _crex crex_.

How to DRAW A Corncrake

Start with a soft pencil. (HB or 2B).

FIG 1

Start with these egg shapes.
Indicate the bill, eyes and
vegetation.

FIG 2

Connect up the egg shapes
as shown.

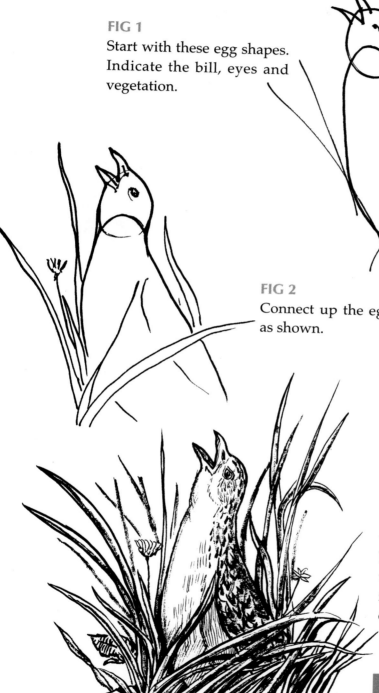

FIG 3

Leave details to the end.
This finished Corncrake
was painted over with a
brush and ink. You can
use a felt-tip marker or
finish it with a pencil. Rub
out any unnecessary lines.

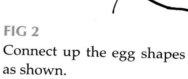

With drawings, you can make
your own Birthday cards,
Wildlife cards, Get Well cards
and Christmas cards.

Peregrine Falcon (Fabhcún gorm)

Male 38cm / Female 48cm

Ireland's largest breeding falcon, this majestic bird is found in wild remote areas nesting on cliff faces and mountain ledges. In the autumn, they move away from their breeding areas to benefit from the greater food supply around our estuaries and even our towns.

A thick-set falcon with broad but pointed wings, it is slate grey in colour and has a broad moustachial stripe. The immature bird is dark brown. The female is larger than the male. Their flight is swift and strong, with fast wing beats. The peregrine is believed to be the fastest moving bird, though this speed is not achieved in direct flight but is when in a stoop (falling steeply on its prey from a great height). A speed of over 130km has been recorded, though it is believed that just over 175km is possible. The male is the better flyer and may reach far greater speeds in a breeding display dive. They feed on a variety of medium-sized birds including duck, waders, seabirds and pigeon species. A pair has successfully nested in Dublin city for several years.

Where: Cliffs, mountains, quarries (estuaries and coastal areas in winter).

Nest: Ledge or crevice on cliff, quarry face or high building.

Eggs: 3 to 4, lightly dappled reddish brown.

Food: Seabirds, pigeons, crows, duck, sometimes grouse.

Voice: Shrill <u>Kek-kek-kek-kek</u>.

Sparrowhawk (Spióróg)

Sparrowhawks are mainly birds of woodland, farmland and hedgerow, but in recent times have nested in cities and towns – mainly in large parks. They are occasionally seen raiding the bird table where small birds are feeding. Often mistaken for a kestrel, the sparrowhawk is more secretive and does not hover. Its wings are shorter and rounder than the kestrel's. It hunts mainly by dashing along a hedgerow, flicking over the top or through a gap and taking a small bird by surprise. It has a very fast flight with short level glides. Sometimes it can be careless when in pursuit of its prey, crashing into windows, wires and other objects. The female sparrowhawk is much larger than the male, is brown in colour, with off-white under-parts barred brown. The male is a neat little bird, with a blue grey colour on his back and head. His front is a warm orange reddish hue with brown barring. Sparrowhawks help keep small bird populations in check as they tend to catch the sickly, the old or the weak. This bird species has been much persecuted over the years, though thankfully, they are now protected by law and their populations are improving.

Where: Conifer and mixed woodland, farmland with hedgerows, large parks.
Nest: Built of sticks. Often adapting an old crow's nest.
Eggs: 4 to 5, whitish.
Food: Small to medium-sized birds.
Voice: Harsh _kek-kek-kek-kek_.

Barn Owl (Scréachóg reilige)

The ghostly hunter of the night, barn owls are most often seen passing over quiet country roads. Their flight is silent. Unfortunately, they are less common in recent times. Barn owls tend to live not too far from human habitation, on farmland and on the outskirts of towns.

They feed mainly on rats and mice. They nest in old farm buildings, ruined castles, old chimneys, and occasionally in hollow trees. They are particularly prone to disturbance which is probably one of the main reasons for the relatively recent decline in their numbers. Barn owls do use nest boxes (see page 46). They breed from April to May, but have been known to nest all the year round. Their eggs are laid at intervals of two days and these hatch after thirty-two days. Delay in egg laying means delay in hatching, so that in years of poor food availability only the larger chicks develop. Young barn owls are fully fledged after three months.

Where: Mainly farmland, meadows, rough grassland close to rivers (a favourite site).

Nest: Old barns, out-buildings, hole in tree, old castle ruins.

Eggs: 4 to 7, white.

Voice: Strangled shriek, hissing, snoring sounds.

Efforts to safeguard and cherish the environment
need to be infused with a vision of the sacred.

Carl Sagan

How to MAKE A Barn Owl Box

Recent years have seen the serious decline of the barn owl in Ireland. One of the reasons is lack of suitable nesting sites. This is where you can help the barn owl – by putting up an artificial nest box. Barn owl nest boxes have proved very successful in Ireland and other parts of the world. The location of these boxes should be in a quiet barn, old castle or large tree. It is important that the location is not disturbed – particularly during the breeding season. It can take some time before the box is used for breeding. However some owls may use the box for roosting. It will be necessary to check the nest box in the autumn in case other birds such as jackdaws have taken it over.

BUILDING A BARN OWL NEST BOX

Tea chests and packing cases can make ideal nest boxes when put indoors, where they will not need to be waterproofed. For outdoor use the box needs to be sturdy and waterproof. It can be any size but the hole entrance should be 150mm wide by 200mm high. The box needs to be at least 750mm deep and needs to be at least 450mm wide and the same in height.

If using a Tea Chest, remember to remove any tin foil and sharp nails.

When constructing the box, help will be needed from an adult, especially when locating it in a barn or tree. Advice should always be sought from a local Wildlife Ranger or Conservation Group member.

— Long-eared Owl (Ceann cait)

36cm

During the winter long-eared owls become more sociable and groups may be seen together. It is a very useful bird on the land as it keeps the rodent population in check.

Where: Woods, copses and plantations.
Nest: Old crow's nest. Occasionally on the ground.
Eggs: 3 to 5, white.
Food: Small mammals and some small birds.
Voice: Low <u>hoot</u>, mewing – sounds like a rusty gate.

The long-eared owl is our most common owl, though seldom seen. A very secretive and nocturnal bird, it is found in woodland copses and at the edges of coniferous forests. Long-eared owls have a beautiful patterned plumage making them extremely difficult to pick out if heard calling from a tree or hedge. Long-eared owls have two techniques to protect themselves from predators. One is to puff themselves up to look bigger and more fearsome than they are, the other is to stretch their bodies and make themselves very slim – to look like part of the tree.

The long-eared owl get its name from the long tufts of feathers (which in fact are not ears) on its head. Its eyes are fiery orange. The long-eared owl does not build a nest but will take over an old crow's nest. It hunts over farmland and rough ground with its ear tufts held flat on its head. Long-eared owls can on occasion be mistaken for our other resident owl, the barn owl.

Long-eared owls are sometimes called wood owls or brown owls.

A wise old owl lived in an oak.
the more he heard the less he spoke.
the less he spoke the more he heard.
O. if men were like that wise bird.

Anonymous

Weather Notes

We all know that the sun, the moon and the weather influence our lives and the lives of all living creatures. Making notes about the weather can be very helpful when looking back on our wildlife experiences. All we have to do is look at the television and listen to the radio, to realise just how influenced we are by the weather. Our weather forecasts are worked out using what can be seen from satellite pictures plus the history of weather details collected from all over the world over the past eighty years. These are computerised and predictions are then made. The sun, the moon and the stars affect not only the weather but also the seasons. Even the wing flap of a tropical butterfly can affect the weather here in Ireland – Yes!! to a tiny degree (it moves the air doesn't it?).

BIRD MIGRATION and THE WEATHER

One of the many wildlife events that is keenly watched in relation to weather patterns is bird migration. In the autumn, when the wind is from the north-west, the Greenland white-fronted geese, who have stopped off in Iceland on their way to Ireland from Greenland, make the most of a 'friendly' wind and are seen arriving for the winter. In the spring the exact opposite happens; when the wind is blowing from the south-east they again make the most of a 'friendly' wind to head back north. During autumn migration many birds are blown off course from the continent by south-easterly winds and this can result in all sorts of unusual birds arriving on our shores.

KEEPING A WEATHER LOG BOOK

You can enter your observations about the weather in a Log Book. Here are some examples of the notes you might keep. Don't forget to add your own remarks for the day.

CLOUD: This is measured in octaves (that is out of 8), for example: 0/8 is no cloud, 4/8 means the sky is half covered and 8/8 means the sky is completely covered with cloud.

WIND DIRECTION: This is the direction from which the wind is coming.

PRECIPITATION: This can be mist, light drizzle, drizzle, light rain, rain or heavy rain.

WIND SPEED IS MEASURED AS FOLLOWS

Force			
	0 = Calm	Smoke rises vertically; water is flat calm	Less than 1 km/h
	1 = Light	Smoke drifts; water has slight ripples	1 – 5 km/h
	2 = Light Breeze	Leaves rustle; water has small wavelets	6 – 11 km/h
	3 = Gentle Breeze	Flags blow straight; large waveletes	12 – 19 km/h
	4 = Moderate breeze	Raises paper and dust; small waves, few 'white horses'	20 – 29 km/h
	5 = Fresh Breeze	Small trees sway; moderate waves, lots of 'white horses'	30 – 39 km/h
	6 = Strong Breeze	Large branches in motion; large waves, some spray	40 – 50 km/h

Force		Description	Speed
7 = Near Gale		Whole trees in motion; large waves, lots of foam	51 – 61 km/h
8 = Gale		Breaks twigs off trees; high waves, foam streaks	62 – 74 km/h
9 = Strong Gale		Slight structural damage; high waves, crests tumbling	75 – 87 km/h
10 = Storm		Trees up-rooted. serious damage; very high waves	88 – 101 km/h
11 = Violent Storm		Widespread damage; waves blown to froth	102 – 115 km/h
12 = Hurricane		Massive damage; water white, driving spray	116 km/h and over

SUNSHINE: Remember when out observing wildlife that the sun's direction has an effect on viewing conditions.

VISIBILITY: Excellent, good, fair or poor.

TEMPERATURE: A rough estimate will do.

REMARKS: A brief summary / synopsis, for example: Mild cloudy morning, heavy rain in the afternoon, clear dry evening.

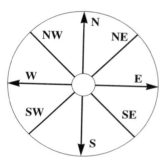

Compass showing the eight main points.

WEATHER AND FOLKLORE
There are many sayings about the weather.

Red sky at night, shepherds' delight. Red sky in the morning, shepherds' warning.
Rain before seven, fine before eleven.
Mackerel sky and mares' tails make tall ships carry sails.
Ring around the moon, the bigger the ring, the nearer the rain.
Fast runs the ant as the mercury rises.
(Referring to the rising barometer – indicating good weather.)

All Creatures obey the Moon's rhythm.
J. Michael Wilson

The right to breathe free is the most basic human right of all.
Rev. Jesse Jackson

Lapwing (Pilibín)

The lapwing is a common and widespread member of the plover family. Its plumage is black and white and it has a greenish sheen. It has a lovely orange colour under the tail (under-tail coverts) and the male's crest is particularly impressive in the breeding season.

During the winter months lapwings can be seen feeding out in fields, by the seashore or on open mud flats. They are useful on the farm because they eat many harmful pests, especially leatherjackets and wireworms.

The nest is a simple scraping in the earth on a slightly elevated site. The eggs are well camouflaged against predators.

During the winter the breeding population in Ireland is joined by lapwings from Europe, with huge numbers arriving, particularly during cold spells. Unfortunately, due to recent changes in farming practices, the breeding population in Ireland has declined.

Where: Wet meadows, moorland, rough pasture.

Nests: Shallow scraping on the ground.

Eggs: Usually 4 (occasionally 2 to 5), buff to brown with black spots and blotches.

Food: Invertebrates, insects and worms.

Voice: Liquid <u>pee-wit</u>.

How to DRAW A Lapwing

O ne of the most attractive birds seen on farmlands and estuaries is the lapwing. Below are some details on how to draw this attractive bird.

FIG 1

Again using your HB or 2B pencil, start with the simple egg shapes. Continue to connect up the lines as shown.

FIG 2

Remember to leave the detail until last. When you are happy that you have the shape and the proportion right, rub out any unnecessary lines.

FIG 3

This finished drawing was completed with brush and ink.

Lapwings are sometimes called peewits or green plovers.

Butterflies and Moths —

The butterfly (Féileacán) and the moth (Féileacán oíche) belong to one of the most colourful and attractive of all our insect orders. The attractiveness of these insects is partly due to their brightly coloured and often distinctively patterned wings which are covered with hundreds of tiny overlapping scales. In comparison to most other insect groups, butterflies are 'normally' relatively simple to identify and are frequently the first indicators of subtle changes in our environment.

Both butterflies and moths belong to the order of insects known as Lepidoptera (which means scaly winged). They can be told apart usually by the difference in their antennae, which for butterflies are club shaped and for moths are feathered or pointed.

Butterflies and moths come under two main headings; Macro, meaning large, which includes all our butterflies and the larger moths, and Micro, which covers the small moths. The identification of the smaller moths is normally only possible using a microscope.

Forty species of butterfly have been recorded in Ireland including six rare migrants, two species that are now extinct and one introduced species. This means that we are dealing with the relatively simple task of the identification of just thirty-one species. With moths, the Irish picture is not so simple as there are around 550 species of large moth and over 700 species of smaller moth!

LIFE CYCLE of the BUTTERFLY and MOTH

Butterflies and moths go through the normal egg, caterpillar (larva), chrysalis (pupa) and adult (imago) forms. The length of these particular stages varies, depending on timing in relation to the availability of the individual species' relevant food-plant. It also depends on when the adult is flying.

SOME RESIDENT BUTTERFLY SPECIES
Wood White (Bánóg choille)

The wood white is a species that is on the wing in May and June along woodland rides and paths. It is our smallest white butterfly and has a particularly weak flight and the unusual habit (for whites) of nearly always resting with its wings closed. The adult never flies far and lives for about two weeks. Eggs are laid singly on the food plant, which is normally bird's-foot trefoil. The eggs hatch between ten to twenty days after laying. The caterpillar feeds for about a month before changing into the chrysalis stage, where it remains for the following ten months.

There is as much to be discovered and to astonish in magnifying an insect as a star.

Thaddeus W. Harris

Small Copper (Copróg bheag)

The small copper is one of our resident butterflies. It is seen from May through to October, but only in small numbers. Eggs, which are laid on sorrel and broad-leaved dock, hatch after about a week. The caterpillar stage lasts from as little as thirty days but can be as long as 145 days when hibernating through the winter. The chrysalis stage is about one month long.

Common Blue (Gormán coiteann)

The common blue is one of our most common butterflies, and believe it or not, is related to the small copper. It can be seen flying from May to as late as October. The primary food plant is bird's-foot trefoil. The eggs hatch in about ten days and the caterpillar is fully grown in about six weeks. They can have up to three broods a year and it is in the last brood stage that they hibernate. The chrysalis stage lasts for about two weeks. Common blues suffer from drought and their population can crash after a dry summer, taking a couple of years to recover.

Small Tortoiseshell (Ruán beag)

The small tortoiseshell is a common, colourful and well-known butterfly. Our resident population is highly mobile, regularly travelling a kilometre or more a day. On occasion, our butterflies are joined by visitors from the continent. Double-brooded, this butterfly is particularly noticeable in the late summer, feeding on nectar from flowers such as buddleia, in preparation for hibernation.

Adults can often be found in our houses during the winter months. Don't disturb them as they are in a deep sleep. Eggs are laid on stinging nettle and hatch in just under a fortnight. The caterpillar feeds for about a month before moving away from its food plant and changing into its chrysalis form which lasts for about two weeks.

Peacock (Péacóg)

The peacock is one of the most spectacular of our butterflies. The adults, whose warning eyes give the butterfly a surprisingly owl-like expression, live for up to eleven months and hibernate in dark

crevices and holes in trees during the winter. Buddleia is particularly attractive to feeding adults. After hibernation eggs are laid on stinging nettle in April and May, and hatch after about a week. The caterpillar form lasts for about a month and the chrysalis stage a further two weeks. The adult insect's dark underwing pattern make it surprisingly difficult to locate when at rest. This butterfly also has the ability to create an audible warning noise by rubbing its forewings and hindwings together.

Wall Brown (Donnóg an bhalla)

The wall brown is found throughout Ireland and is more common on its second emergence when up to three times the number of adults may be seen flying. Very much a sun-loving butterfly, this double-brooded species is regularly seen basking with its wings outstretched. The adult male lives for about three days. Eggs are laid close to a wide variety of wild grasses and they hatch after about ten days. The caterpillar changes to its chrysalis form after a month, and after a period of time emerges as a butterfly.

THE MIGRANT BUTTERFLY SPECIES
Clouded Yellow (Buíóg chróch)

The clouded yellow is one of our most spectacular and rare migrants from North Africa and the continent. Periodically there are particularly good clouded yellow years. These periods can be quite spectacular with

large numbers of these pretty butterflies arriving on our shores.

Red Admiral (Aimiréal dearg)

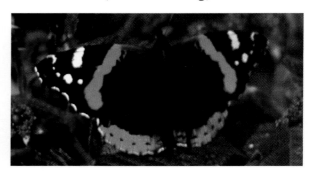

The red admiral is a fairly common migrant from the continent and is seen from April throughout the summer. Eggs are laid on stinging nettles and hatch after about a week. The caterpillar feeds for about four weeks before entering the chrysalis stage. The butterfly emerges after a further two to three weeks. Warm summers seem to suit red admirals which can often be seen feeding on buddleia.

Painted Lady (Áilleán)

The painted lady is a migrant to Ireland from Europe and North Africa. It arrives from May and has the ability to reproduce quite quickly in warm weather with the egg, caterpillar and chrysalis stages being completed in as little as a month. The eggs are usually laid on thistles. None normally survive the winter.

> Two species of butterfly from America have been recorded: American painted lady and monarch.

MOTHS and THEIR CATERPILLARS

Moths are both fascinating and beautiful creatures, often overlooked or not liked, which is a great pity. Most of our moth species tend to fly by night. Different species can be seen throughout the year. One of the best ways of observing them is at an outside light. A moth trap can be used if you want to make a study of them. These traps are set at night and emptied of their catches the following morning. A large white sheet of paper laid on the ground can also work. You will be amazed at the diversity of colour, pattern and size of these somehow particularly exciting insects, which we rarely come across in our normal day-to-day lives.

Six-spot Burnet (Buirnéad sébhallach)

The six-spot burnet is a resident moth regularly seen on the wing during sunshine in the months of June to August. The species is recognised by the six bright pinkish spots on each forewing. Its main food plant is bird's-foot trefoil. It winters as a caterpillar.

Eyed Hawk-moth

The eyed hawk-moth is a scarce resident with spectacular large 'peacock-like' eyes in the hind wings which are used for frightening potential predators. When threatened, the adult has a habit of vibrating its wings which is really quite scaring. Normally single-brooded, it can be seen flying at night from May to July. The caterpillar's food plants include willow. Winter is spent in the chrysalis stage.

Elephant Hawk-moth (Conach eilifinteach)

The elephant hawk-moth is another large and local resident. Its brilliant pinkish coloration is unmistakable. The caterpillar feeds on a number of plants including willowherb and bedstraw. Winter is spent in the chrysalis form.

Burnished Brass (Prásach)

The burnished brass is a common resident, easily recognised by its glistening greenish-gold colour from which it gets its name. Single and occasionally double-brooded, this moth can be found flying from June to July and sometimes in August and September. Food plants include buddleia, valerian and thistles. Winter is spent as a caterpillar.

Buff Tip (Rinnbhuí)

The buff tip is a common resident that flies in June and July. This spectacular moth looks just like a broken twig as it rests up for the day. The caterpillar feeds on a variety of food plants.

Pale Prominent (Starraicín)

The pale prominent is a common resident that flies during May and June and, when double brooded, in August. The food plants of the caterpillar are poplar and willow. They can be easily overlooked because of their excellent camouflage.

Poplar Hawk-moth (Conach)

The poplar hawk-moth is one of our most common hawk-moths and can be seen flying mainly in May and June. It gets its name from the poplar tree on which the caterpillar feeds.

The exceptional position of man in the world of creation gives him no excuse for treating the world of nature in an absolute and irresponsible way.

Fr. Jan Grzesica

Breeding Butterflies

It is possible to collect caterpillars or eggs from hedgerows or trees in spring or autumn time (only take a few). Bring them home in a container and make sure to take some of the plant that they were on. Small caterpillars are best kept in a fish tank type container (as illustrated). You can buy these in a pet shop or try to make your own using clear perspex with a very fine mesh lid on top.

Make sure that there is a regular supply of fresh food. As the leaves turn yellowish replace them with fresh ones. Be careful not to throw out the caterpillars with the leaves as some caterpillars blend in very well with their food plant. If you need to transfer caterpillars from one container to another, you can use a small, soft paintbrush. They will climb on to the bristles and in that way can be transferred safely.

After a time you will notice that your caterpillars stop feeding. This is the time when they may change their skin. This can happen four to five times in a caterpillar's life – these different stages are called 'instars'. Some butterfly caterpillars pupate at the base of the plant – this involves them hanging from a twig. Twigs or pieces of bark standing up will be useful in helping the caterpillar achieve this stage. Some may remain for a long time in the pupate stage. Usually those that pupate in the spring will emerge later in the year. Those that do not, should be kept in a cool place – such as a shed or garage – during the winter. Sprinkle these occasionally with water. With any luck you will witness the amazing spectacle of the adult pulling itself from the pupae, climbing up a twig and drying out its crumpled wings. Release the flying adults where you collected the caterpillars or at some other similar and suitable habitat.

BEWARE
Some caterpillars can cause irritation to skin, so handling should be avoided.

Amazing Bird Facts

LARGEST BIRD IN IRELAND
The mute swan male weighs 12 to 14kg. Its length, which is half head and neck is 1.5m, its wingspan is 2m. (The great bustard, which is bigger, has been recorded in Ireland – two in Thurles, Co. Tipperary in 1902 and a female shot near Castletownbere, Co. Cork in 1925.)

LARGEST BIRD IN THE WORLD
The male African ostrich weighs up to 150kg and stands up to 2.5m.

LARGEST FLYING BIRD IN EUROPE
The male great bustard often reaches 16.5kg and stands over 1m with a wingspan of 2.5m.

SMALLEST BIRD IN IRELAND
The goldcrest and the firecrest (a rare migrant) are the same size. The wren is slightly larger and weighs twice as much as the goldcrest.

SMALLEST BIRD IN THE WORLD
The bee hummingbird is 5.7cm long and weighs 1.6g.

DEEPEST DIVER IN THE WORLD
The Emperor penguin dives to a depth of 265m in 18mins.

DEEPEST DIVER IN IRELAND
The great northern diver dives to a depth of 81m.

MOST AERIAL LAND-BIRD IN IRELAND
The common swift flies for up to three years on its maiden voyage. When it leaves the nest for the first time, it has no need to land again until it returns to breed. It eats, drinks and sleeps on the wing.

MOST AERIAL BIRD IN THE WORLD
The sooty tern stays aloft from three to ten years.

LONGEST LIVED CAPTIVE BIRD
'Cocky' the sulphur crested cockatoo died at the age of eighty-two in London Zoo.

SHORTEST LIFE EXPECTANCY
One of the shortest lived birds is the robin with a live expectancy of five to six months.

LONGEST LIVED WILD BIRD
The royal albatross can live for over fifty-eight years.

WORLD'S RECORDED HIGHEST FLYER
A Ruppel's griffon vulture flew at 11,274m (37,000 feet) on 29 November 1973 and collided with a commercial aircraft over the Ivory Coast of Africa

IRELAND'S RECORDED HIGHEST FLYER
A whooper swan flew at 8,230m (27,000 feet) on 9 December 1967 and was seen by a pilot flying at that altitude over the Inner Hebrides of Scotland.

MOST FEATHERS
The highest number of feathers was on a whistling swan (N. American relation of the Bewick's swan). Of the 25,216 feathers, 80% were on the head and neck. The whistling swan has been recorded in Ireland.

WORLD'S FASTEST FLYING BIRD
In straight steady flight the eider duck is currently believed to be the fastest flying bird having been recorded at 76km/h.

LARGEST EGG SIZE LAID IN IRELAND
The mute swan lays eggs approximately 11.5cm long by 7.4cm wide.

SMALLEST EGG SIZE LAID IN IRELAND
The goldcrest lays eggs approximately 13mm long by 9.5mm wide.

Reference: Martin, B.P. 1987. World Birds. Guinness Superlatives Ltd.

Photo Quiz 1

1.

2.

3.

4.

5.

6.

7.

8.

Bottle-nosed Dolphin (Dorad)

2.5m to 3.5m

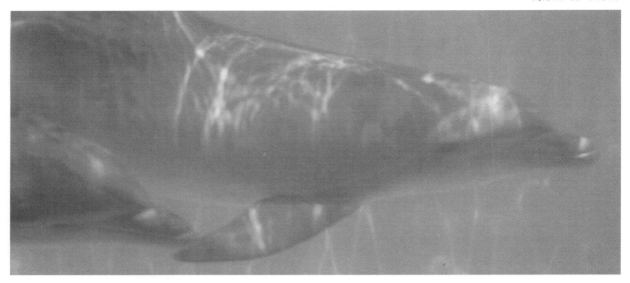

Many people will be familiar with the bottled-nosed dolphin from television shows like *Flipper*, and our resident Dingle dolphin, Fungie. Bottled-nosed dolphins are usually seen in small groups feeding together. Curious by nature, dolphins will come to investigate boats and ships. They seem to be unafraid of humans and many people have enjoyed swimming with them, some even claiming to have had healing experiences from depression or loneliness.

Dolphins live for up to thirty years, maturing at the age of six. When dolphins breed, young are born twelve months later. Other female dolphins will help the mother during delivery – a bit like our mid-wives do in hospitals. The young are weaned after two years. A mother may have up to eight calves in her lifetime.

Dolphins use echolocation to locate their prey. One of the reasons why dolphins are so successful is because they eat a variety of foods. Mullet, ray, eels, shrimps and crabs all form part of their diet. Dolphins will sometimes follow trawlers taking advantage of the fish stirred up by the nets.

The biggest threats to these magnificent creatures are pollution, a decline in much of their fish stocks and being hunted by man. They also run the risk of being taken from the wild and put on display to the public. Ireland has made its waters a 'Whale and Dolphin Sanctuary' which is great news for us and for these remarkable cetaceans.

Where: Common in coastal waters. Has been known to go up rivers and enter estuaries.
Food: Fish, eels, crabs, shrimps.
Description: Robust, yet streamlined. Grey colour on back and light grey on flanks and belly. Broad dorsal fin, curves backwards along the centre of the back. Stubby beak, with flippers and fluke (tail).

Grey Seal (Rón glas)

Male 3.2m / Female 2.5m

Common all around the Irish coastline, they prefer a breeding site facing the Atlantic Ocean. Coat colour is variable. The bull (male) is black to mid-grey and is darker than the cow (female) who is lighter in colour with an overall spotted coat. Seals are mature at six years but do not normally breed until their tenth year.

Dominant bulls have harems of about ten cows and breeding takes place in late autumn when the bull finds a suitable site. Pups are born in September or October, with one pup per family. Seals feed on fish, crabs and lobsters. The grey seal has a more pointed head than the common seal (common seals have a more cat-like face and their young are dark in colour).

Where: Spends most of its life at sea.

Breeding: Breeding colonies (rookeries) mostly on small rocky islands.

Young: The pup has a white coat which is shed after three weeks.

Food: Fish, crabs and lobsters.

Frog (Frog)

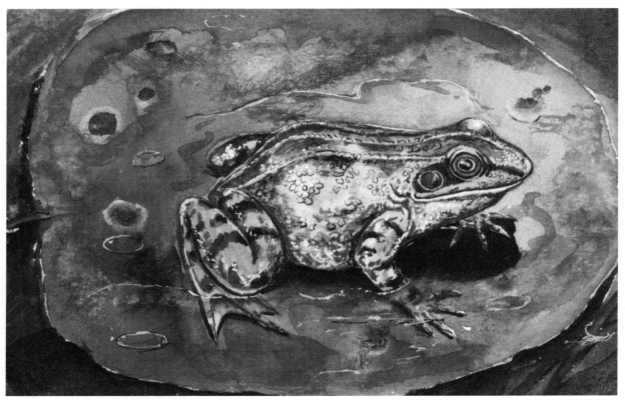

The frog is our most familiar amphibian, and is widely distributed throughout Ireland. It is believed to have been introduced into Ireland in Norman times, possibly for food. Frogs become particularly active from late January through to February.

Shallow pools, ponds and ditches are regularly used to spawn in and tadpoles develop quickly from the egg stage. It takes a frog one to two years to become fully mature and full adult life can last for about seven years. Frogs are easily recognised, though colour does vary from a pale yellowish to dark purplish colour.

Frogs are useful to the gardener as they eat beetles, caterpillars, flies, slugs and snails.

There are a number of legends associated with frogs, one being the belief that to cure toothache you have to keep the frog alive in your mouth until it has croaked three times – Ugh! We certainly do not recommend this!

Where: Widespread in ponds, ditches, streams, bogs etc.
Breeding: January – February. Frog spawn found in many ponds and small pools.
Young: Tadpoles develop into small frogs.
Food: Beetles, caterpillars, flies, slugs and snails.

Natterjack Toad (Cnádán)

The natterjack is the only toad species in Ireland and is easily recognised by the yellow stripe that runs down its back. This stripe is part of its camouflage, being a replica of the sand sedge which is a common plant in this toad's habitat. Natterjack toads can be found in south Co. Kerry and also at a site in Co. Wexford, where they have been re-located to reduce the risk of them becoming extinct in Ireland. The natterjack toad does not appear until near the end of April. Like other toads, it has a warty skin.

One interesting and noticeable feature is that it runs rather than hops. In the spring, when the male is most active, the loud croaking call can be heard from as much as one kilometre away. Natterjack toad spawn is laid in distinctive strings in ponds found in dune slacks, one of their preferred habitats.

The natterjack toad was first recorded in Ireland in 1805. It is not known whether it is a native species or whether it was introduced to the south-west just over 200 years ago.

Where:	Co. Kerry in sandy and bog type locations, also in Co. Wexford.
Breeding:	April.
Young:	Tadpoles develop into small toads.
Food:	Invertebrates.

Smooth Newt (Earc sléibhe)

up to 100mm

The smooth (or common) newt, is Ireland's only tailed amphibian (the common lizard being a reptile). Although a native member of our fauna, it is relatively under-recorded. This is probably partly due to its elusive nature and also because it is regularly mistaken for a lizard. It breeds, from February, in weeded ponds and the female lays her eggs singularly, attaching them to underwater vegetation.

Newts do not have territories, though the male does need some time to reach breeding condition. Newts spend up to four months of the year in water. The male has large black belly spots, whereas the female has a speckled belly. During the breeding season the male develops a crest along his back and the belly becomes a rich orange. Newts engage in elaborate courtship dances during breeding. Tadpoles develop into small newts. Maturity takes about eighteen months.

There are various legends relating to newts. One involves the newt running down the throat of an open-mouthed sleeper and then being enticed back out with bowls of porridge. Another is that they will run down your throat if you drink pond water.

The newt was widely believed to help cure burns. Someone who had licked the belly of a newt, would then cure the burns by licking them. More activities which we definitely do not recommend!

Where: Widespread, but not very common.

Breeding: From February. Eggs laid individually under a leaf.

Young: Tadpoles develop into small newts.

Food: Invertebrates.

Common Lizard (Eare luachra)

up to 180mm

Common (or viviparous) lizards are normally brown or yellowish in colour with black stripes running along the back. They love the sun and will often be seen basking on open bare ground or on a rock. When disturbed they run away and often it is the quick rustle as they disappear under cover that is the only sign of an encounter.

They are found all over Ireland although records are sketchy, with more being seen around our coasts. The common lizard, unlike most other reptiles, does not lay eggs, but gives birth to live young. (Viviparous means bringing forth live young, not from an egg.) A litter can contain up to twelve young. Males reach maturity in their second year while the females take a year longer.

Where: Widespread, but not very common. More seen around coasts. They like cliffs, dunes, bogs, embankments and walls.

Young: Give birth to live young that look like tiny replicas of their parents.

Food: Invertebrates.

Ladybird (Ciaróg na mbeannacht) — 6mm

Ladybirds, like butterflies and bees, are welcome visitors to the garden. They are easily identified because of their bright colours and spots. Ladybirds are well known to most people. In Ireland and Britain, where there are over forty-five different species. The 'seven spot' is the most common of the ladybird species. The gardener's friend, the seven-spot ladybird helps to keep down destructive aphids. This beetle gets its name from the middle ages, when for some reason it was associated with the Blessed Virgin and its old name was Beetle of Our Lady.

When displayed on insects, red is one of nature's warning colours, telling predators not to eat them. If a bird eats one of these beetles it gets an unpleasant taste and so learns to avoid them. In winter, ladybirds shelter in large communities behind the bark of, or inside, a tree. In spring they search out plants that have aphids on them, for example nettles and rose bushes. There they mate and the female lays up to fifty eggs at a time. All ladybirds are carnivorous with the exception of the 24-spot ladybird which eats mainly clover.

Where:	Widespread.
Breeding:	Late spring. Lays up to fifty eggs on nettles and rose bushes.
Young:	Larva are carnivores and feed on aphids. Pupates on food plant.
Food:	Aphids.

Honey Bee (Beach mheala)

12mm

These very useful insects have been kept in hives by humans for thousands of years. No doubt you have enjoyed the fruits of the bee's labour – namely honey. The honey bee is a social insect. Colonies can have up to 8,000 bees in them. The queen bee lays up to a 1,000 eggs a day. She is larger than the others and they are all subordinate to her. Females are called 'workers' and males are 'drones'.

When bees find suitable nectar, they will return to the hive and do a dance around the comb. This is a clockwise or anti-clockwise dance. If the source of food is further away than 100m, a worker will dance a number 8 shape, then waggling her abdomen across the shape she indicates the direction. Pollen from flowers is placed on the bee's back leg and carried back to the hive. The workers then take it and by chewing convert it into nectar (honey).

The nest is built with wax produced by the workers in a hexagonal pattern design, to avoid any wasted space. There are worker cells, drone cells, honey stores and queen cells. When the queen grows old, a new queen emerges from a separate part of the hive. She attacks the old queen cells killing the occupants. Then she takes flight to mate with the drones, who die shortly afterwards. She returns to the nest (and may even kill the old queen) and her reign will then begin.

The honey bee is probably at the top of the list of most useful insects to humans.

Where:	Widespread.
Breeding:	Man-made and natural hives. Queen is integral to the success of the hive.
Young:	Larvae. Each type of bee has its own special function.
Food:	Nectar from flowers.

Cross Spider (Damhán garraí)

The cross (or common garden) spider is recognised by the cross-shaped pattern on its abdomen. Abundant in gardens, on fences and in hedgerows, it generally rests on a nearby leaf. This spider makes a large orb web that adorns trees and shrubs in summer. They become particularly noticeable when they have had a good meal as their abdomen swells up, highlighting the cross pattern.

Spiders are not insects but belong to the class Arachnida, having four pairs of legs, no wings or antennae and simple rather than compound eyes. The spider's body is divided into two sections. The front section is where the legs, the chelicerae (the jaws) and the pedipalps (the 'hands') are attached. Spiders are armed with poisoned fangs to subdue prey and deter predators. The rear section, or abdomen, is where they produce silk from spinners to make a web that will trap their prey. They will repair any damage to the web and sometimes will eat the web before re-building it.

WHY DID THE FLY FLY? BECAUSE THE SPIDER SPIED HER.

Not all spiders make webs, though all produce silk which may be used as a safety line, or to wrap up their eggs.

Where: Abundant in gardens, fences and hedgerows.
Breeding: Generally under a nearby leaf. Eggs are protected in a silk-spun egg sack.
Food: Small insects caught in web.

Dragonflies and Damselflies

2 to 7cm

Brown hawker

The Dragonfly (Snáthaid mhór) and damselfly (Béchuil) are among the most beautiful of our insects. Adult dragonflies are large, heavily built, powerful predators, whereas the damselflies tend to be more dainty. Dragonflies tend to rest with their wings open, whereas damselflies usually close their wings over the back. Both are the hawks of the insect world and they feed on other insects which they catch, usually on the wing. With large compound eyes and four translucent wings, dragonflies and damselflies belong to a group of insects called Odonata which is Greek for 'toothed jaws'.

The females lays their eggs in water while hovering close to the surface. An aquatic nymph hatches out from the egg. These nymphs are also fierce carnivorous predators, catching invertebrates and worms. After about a year in the water, the fully grown nymph climbs out onto a piece of nearby vegetation. The body splits and a four-winged adult insect climbs out, dries itself in the sun and then flies off.

Where:	Widespread. Usually hunt near and over water.
Breeding:	During spring and summer. Female lays eggs in water.
Young:	Aquatic nymph which is a fierce predator.
Food:	Invertebrates and worms.

69

Kerry Slug (Drúchtín an Ciarraí)

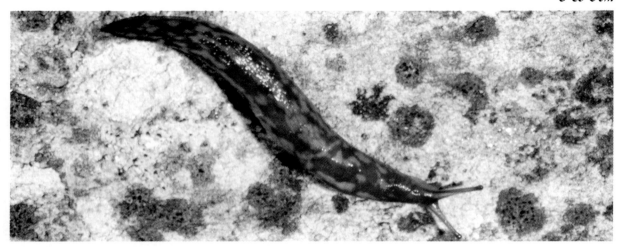

The Kerry slug is confined to the extreme south-west of Ireland, being found only in Co. Cork and Co. Kerry. This species of slug is also recorded in Spain and Portugal and there are old records in Brittany, though not since 1868. Slugs and snails are part of one of the largest animal groups, the Mollusca, which have over 80,000 species in the world. They are distinguished from other animals, by their muscular 'foot', and the presence of a mantle protecting their internal organs.

The difference between slugs and snails is not as straight-forward as one might imagine. The word snail can include slugs in the general term, though normally we refer to snails as those that are able to get inside their shell and slugs as those animals without a shell (or in possession of a minute shell – often not visible as it is actually inside the slug). The Kerry slug is a large slug with a greenish grey body and yellowish white spotting. The sole of the Kerry slug is creamy and the mucus (slime) is colourless to milky in colour. They like lichen and moss-covered rocks and trees. Kerry slugs are very hard to find in dry weather, though careful searching in damp drains and other moist areas can prove fruitful. One of the easiest ways of identifying this species is by its unusual habit of rolling into a ball when attacked (this is not done by other slugs). One of the most common predators of all slugs and snails is the song thrush.

Where:	South-west of Ireland in Co. Kerry and Co. Cork.
Home:	Likes lichen and moss-covered rocks and trees. Can be found in damp drains. Does not like dry periods.
Food:	Herbivore. Eats a wide range of plants, rotting vegetation, fungi, algae and lichens.
Breeding:	Hermaphrodite which means they are both male and female. They normally lay eggs about two weeks after mating, though they can delay egg laying for up to a year. Eggs, which are laid in the soil, hatch after about six weeks.
Young:	Miniature copies of the adult, taking anything from one to two years to mature.

Photo Quiz 2

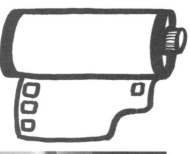

Answers

1. Tree sparrow   2. Bee orchid   3. Crossbill   4. Sparrowhawk chick   5. Harebells   6. Green tiger beetle

71

Rabbit (Coinín)

Smaller than the hare, the rabbit is usually sandy to brown (with no dark ear tips). Black rabbits are common in certain areas. The white underside of its tail is always visible as it runs away. Rabbits were introduced to Ireland in the twelfth century by the Normans. They are widespread in grasslands and scrubby places including sand dunes and open woodlands. They live in underground colonies known as warrens and are active mainly at night.

Rabbits feed on grasses, but will eat cereal crops, roots, and young trees. They breed between January and June and up to eight young are born a month after mating. Rabbits can breed in their first year.

Where:	*Widespread.*
Home:	*Underground warren. Some areas are occupied for generations. These are usually located where the land slopes gently.*
Food:	*Herbivore. Eats a wide range of plant food.*
Breeding:	*Prolific. Rabbits produce three to five litters of seven young per year.*
Young:	*Young, known as kittens, are born blind and naked.*

Irish Hare (Giorria Éireannach)

50 to 60cm

There are two kinds of hare found in Ireland; the Irish or mountain hare, and the brown hare (introduced from Britain and very rare). The Irish hare is more heavily built than the brown hare. Its summer coat is reddish brown and it turns paler in winter. The ears have black tips. Our Irish hare does not turn completely white in winter as they do in Scotland and other parts of Europe. The Irish hare lives above ground in a form (a shallow surface shelter). They are common in many parts of Ireland.

The hare feeds mainly at night on grasses and heather. The young are called leverets and there may be up to three litters a year. An Irish hare eats approximately 500g of food a day.

Where: Widespread.

Home: Form made in grass (do not dig burrows). Will shelter in clumps of grass, field edges (headlands), and beside hedges and ditches.

Food: Grasses, herbs, heather and other vegetation.

Breeding: Most active breeding occurs in the spring. Up to three litters in a season, producing 2 to 4 young in a litter. Young, known as leverets, are well developed at birth, fully furred and their eyes are open.

The World of Bats

The bat (Ialtóg) is the only mammal capable of true flight. Bats are particularly skilful and agile and are able to manoeuvre accurately at low speeds. They feed mainly on small flies and moths. Their wings are a thin skin supported by their specially-adapted elongated arms and their second, third, fourth and fifth fingers. The skin is also attached to the body and legs and often extends between the legs, attaching to the tail. Just the thumb is clawed and this, along with the toes, is used for gripping and hanging.

During the day bats may rest in a variety of roosting places, such as caves, crevices, hollow trees and in buildings. In summer, they tend to leave their roost sites to feed just before dusk, and are particularly active during the early part of the night.

> Insect-eating bats are helpful to humans, and many bat species around the world play an important role in plant pollination and seed dispersal.

ECHOLOCATION

Bats navigate and target their prey by echolocation. This is done by the bat producing a high pitched sound that is reflected back as an echo from the surrounding surfaces (and even the hunted insect) to a bat's ears. The echo is used by the bat to create a 'hearing picture' of the surrounding area. Each species of bat produces this sound in its own particular way so that, with the aid of a special bat receiver, we can identify the species of bat flying. Of the 850 to 900 bats species in the world, just seven occur in Ireland.

HIBERNATION

Bats hibernate in the winter, as their food supply of insects becomes scarce. They normally hibernate in special winter roost sites which may be a cave, a mine or even a cellar. Bats can travel hundreds of kilometres to these special sites where they undergo elaborate changes in their body system so that they can survive the winter months without eating. During this hibernation period, bats are very vulnerable as their body temperature drops from around 37°C to about 10°C and their heartbeat drops from several hundred beats per minute down to about ten beats per minute. If bats are disturbed during the winter months they run the risk of dying.

WHY DAMP ROOSTS?

Bats are particularly prone to dehydration as they have an enormous skin area in comparison to their size. This is why they hunt mainly at night and are found in cool dark places such as cellars, caves, mineshafts etc . . .

BREEDING CYCLE

A female bat produces just one young in the year. She does not make a nest but chooses a warm, clean, dark location to rear her offspring. This spot is called a nursery roost and is normally made in a bridge, a building, a cave, a church or a suitable tree. The male plays no part in the rearing of the baby and roosts in a different place.

Bat watching is best about fifteen minutes before sunset.

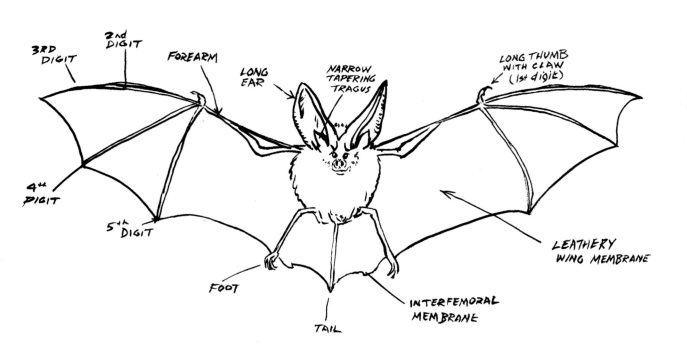

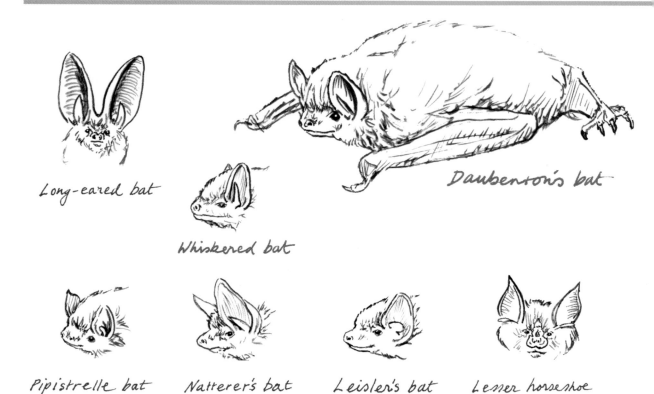

Long-eared bat

Whiskered bat

Daubenton's bat

Pipistrelle bat   Natterer's bat   Leisler's bat   Lesser horseshoe

BATS of the WORLD

Bats species are broken into two groups: the Megabats, which include the larger bats with the biggest bat living in Java and having a wingspan of 1.7m and a body length of 42cm; and the Microbats, which include the smallest bat in the world, the Kitti's hog-nosed bat of Thailand, which is just 29mm to 33mm long and weighs about 2g.

BATS of IRELAND

The seven species of bat in Ireland belong to the Microbat group, with the pipistrelle being both Europe's and Ireland's smallest bat with a body length of between 33mm and 52mm and a weight of between 3g and 8g.

Pipistrelle Bat (Ialtóg fheascrach)

This is our most common bat and the smallest (small enough to fit in a matchbox). One pipistrelle will eat up to 3,000 midges in a single night!

Lesser Horseshoe Bat (Crú-ialtóg bheag)

This bat's range is confined to the west and south-west of Ireland. Our population is of international importance.

Whiskered Bat (Ialtóg ghiobach)

Uncommon and rare, this bat is distributed over the whole of Ireland.

Natterer's Bat (Ialtóg Natterer)

This bat is relatively common and widely distributed.

Daubenton's Bat (Ialtóg Dhaubenton)

A common bat, it is often seen feeding over open water.

Long-eared Bat (Ialtóg chluasach)

Common throughout, this bat is the easiest species to identify due to its large ears, which are three quarters of the combined length of its head and body .

Leisler's Bat (Ialtóg Leisler)

This bat is common throughout the country. Ireland is the European stronghold for this species.

OLD SUPERSTITIONS

It was believed that when the devil wasn't tormenting people, he would take the form of a bat and fly about. In eastern European traditions, vampires could change themselves into bats. In Ireland people believed that ghosts could enter houses in the disguise of a bat.

BATS and THE LAW

Bats are a protected species in Ireland and Britain and most other countries. This means that we must not interfere with their roosts or breeding sites.

Sadly, bat numbers have been in decline in recent years. This is primarily due to two reasons: insect numbers and suitable sites.

1. Insect numbers are lower due to the use of modern chemical insecticide sprays.
2. There are fewer suitable places for bats to roost and breed. Modern buildings and bridges do not have the same number of nooks and crannies that older buildings once had.

HELPING BATS

You can encourage bats by making a bat box, which is similar to a bird box except that the entrance is at the bottom. These can be placed in shaded areas on trees and old walls.

The Wild Beauty of Bogs

In Ireland we don't have rain forests, savannahs, or prairies, but we are lucky to still have boglands. For centuries these areas were associated with poverty and bad lands, or simply a place to cut fuel for the fire. In recent years with the loss of many of these wild places due to burning or draining, people are becoming more aware of the importance of bogs. Poets, artists, writers and sculptors have always drawn inspiration from these wonderful places.

Nowadays scientists, botanists, geologists, historians, conservationists and ornithologists have voiced their concerns for the need to preserve these rich tapestries of plant, insect, bird, and mammal life. Sensitive tourists come to Ireland just to walk these bogs, which as a habitat are becoming increasingly rarer world wide. Although there is a greater appreciation of the fauna and flora of these bogs, it is a sad fact that many are still threatened by commercial interests. Bogs that have been in Ireland for over 5,000 years can be destroyed in just a few weeks.

It is important that we save these bogs so that future generations may experience their wild beauty.

Snipe

Great sundew

For centuries humans have been trying to tame and control nature as if they were outside or separated from it. Thankfully these attitudes are changing. Instead of competing with nature, now we are willing to learn from her. By doing this, wildlife and human life can flourish alongside each other.

Bladderwort

The World of Crows

The crow (préachán) family causes extreme reactions among people. People either love or loathe them. Down through the centuries, crows have had a chequered history. Ravens were always considered birds of ill omen because of their unfortunate habit of feeding on dead men who were hanged by the roadside. People thought they were agents of the devil that had come to take away the person's soul. On the other hand the raven was considered a royal bird and to this day ravens can be found at the Tower of London. The North American Indians considered the raven a messenger from the spirit world.

Magpies probably cause the most negative reactions in people, with the superstition that one magpie brings bad luck, and the belief that magpies clear all the gardens and hedgerows of small birds. Rooks, which are the farmer's friend, were considered a sign of good luck if nesting in a rookery on your land and if they left, bad luck would befall the area. Jackdaws were considered thieves and they were also encouraged to speak. Unfortunately this was done by splitting the bird's tongue.

> Crows are considered the most intelligent of all the bird families. They can actually count to two.

CROW SPECIES in IRELAND
In Ireland we have ravens, hooded crows, rooks, choughs, magpies, jays and jackdaws.

> Crows were considered pests and as a result the scarecrow was invented.

Raven (Fiach dubh)

The raven is the most widespread and largest member of the crow family.

Hooded Crow (Feannóg)

The hooded crow is common on farmland, bogland and coastal areas. In the midlands they can be seen roosting in large flocks.

Chough (Cág cosdearg)

The chough is particularly attractive with its bright red down-curved bill and red legs. It is found mainly in coastal locations.

Jackdaw (Cág)

The jackdaw is common and is our smallest crow.

Rook (Rúcach)

The rook is widespread in Ireland and nests in large rookeries.

Rookery

The word 'rookery' is used for some other colony species such as penguins and seals.

Jay (scréachóg)

The jay is mainly found in woodland areas. A shy and wary bird, it is often glimpsed as it flies away. A particularly distinctive feature is its white rump.

The jay is known as 'the guardian of the woods' because of its alarm call when somebody approaches.

Magpie (Snag breac)

The magpie is common and easily identified. It was first recorded in Ireland in Co. Wexford in 1676.

The wounds we have inflicted on the earth can be healed . . . But if it is to be done it must be done now, otherwise, it may never be done at all.'

Jonathan Porritt

Gannet (Gainéad)

In flight the gannet shows long narrow wings and a pointed streamlined tail. The adult plumage is white with a buff head and nape, and black wing tips. The immature gannets have dark plumage with white specks. They become whiter as they mature.

Gannets are a spectacular sight when hunting for fish, diving from heights of 30m, their wings swept back while breaking the water.

Gannets nest in large colonies called a gannetry, which may contain as many as 60,000 pairs. The nests consist of large heaps of seaweed and other plants as well as discarded materials such as rope and nylon netting. The clutch is normally a single egg and the chick hatches after about forty days. Gannets move out to sea after the breeding season.

Where: Rocky islands. Seen out at sea off all coasts.

Nest: Heaps of seaweed, vegetation and clay. Nest in noisy gannetry.

Eggs: 1 to 2, chalky pale blue.

Food: Fish, especially mackerel and herring.

Voice: Loud grating call.

Shag (Seaga)

Shags have a somewhat prehistoric look about them as do their relations – the cormorants. Shags are smaller than cormorants with a scaly black plumage that has an iridescent green hue. In the breeding season the male has a prominent crest and the bill has a noticeable yellow gape which disappears in winter. In flight the wing beats are slightly faster than those of the cormorant.

When diving the shag will normally make a distinct leap out of the water before submerging (cormorants being bigger, do not tend to do this). Shags stay under water for about thirty seconds before reappearing. Their nests are on sheltered undisturbed cliff ledges or rocky islands. Shags are strictly coastal in distribution, whereas cormorants can be seen inland on lakes and along rivers.

Where: Rocky coasts and small islands.
Nest: Heap of weeds and bits of vegetation, built on sheltered ledges and under rocks.
Eggs: Usually 3, pale blue/chalky white.
Food: Fish.
Voice: Grunts and clicks.

Puffin (Puifin)

30cm

The puffin is a rather comical-looking member of the auk family. In summer their plumage is black, with a white belly, orange legs, pale grey face and a large multicoloured bill. In winter the bill sheds its colourful outer shell, and the puffins appear more auk-like and less clownish. Skilled fliers and fishers, puffins actually 'fly' underwater to catch fish. They can hold several fish at once in their parrot-like beaks. Their webbed feet are only used to swim at the surface. They live in a burrow which is taken over from rabbits or excavated on grass plateaus above sea cliffs and on islands.

When returning to their nests, they fly in big circles, just off shore, to evade predatory gulls that wait to dash them to the ground as they try to land. One egg is laid in early May and it hatches after 39 days. The young have brown downy feathers and have a small bill. The parents feed the young for about forty days, after which the young puffin must make its own way to the sea. Puffins spend the winter at sea.

Where: Sea cliffs and islands during breeding season. Out at sea in winter.
Nest: Burrows in grassy sea-cliffs and banks.
Egg: 1 to 2, usually white.
Young: Cared for by both parents. Makes its own way off the cliff and into the sea.
Food: Sand eels and small fish.

Grey Heron (Corr réise)

90cm

Herons nest in colonies (or heronry) in trees. Four to five pale greenish-blue eggs are laid in a nest built by the female.

Present all year round, the grey heron is seen along the seashore, around lakes and in river estuaries.

Where: Rivers, lakes, marshes, bogs, coastal areas (especially in winter).

Nest: A large stick construction in the trees (will occasionally nest on the ground).

Eggs: 4 to 5, pale blue.

Food: Fish, small mammals and birds, frogs, eels.

Voice: Harsh, loud <u>frank</u> call. Young give a loud squeal.

Alert and motionless in shallow water, the watchful heron waits patiently for a fish or some small creature to come within range of its dagger-sharp bill. Then it strikes, stabbing the prey and swallowing it whole.

The grey heron is a large long-legged and long-necked bird, with a white head and dark streaks on the neck. Its yellow bill becomes a bright pink colour during the breeding season.

In Elizabethan England the grey heron was known as 'the handsaw'.

I know a hawk from a handsaw.
Hamlet: William Shakespeare

Mute Swan (Eala bhalbh)

The mute swan is the largest of our birds and is easily recognisable by its white plumage. Mute swans are common on canals, rivers, lakes and estuaries. Despite its name the mute swan is not silent but gives occasional guttural, grunting and hissing noises. The young (called cygnets) are more vocal. The adult male is called a cob and the female a pen. Adults have an orange/red bill with a black knob at the base.

Because of its size a swan is slow to get airborne, usually taking a long run at it. However once in the air they are very graceful, although they have difficulty manoeuvring quickly away from overhanging wires and the like. Their wings make a loud humming or whistling sound.

A swan's nest consists of a large heap of vegetation with a depression in the centre. Cygnets are downy grey/brown in colour and they attain their full adult plumage over a period of two to three years.

The swan winters on open waters and along the coast.

Where: Shallow waters, lakes, canals, rivers, estuaries, sheltered coasts.

Nest: A big heap of vegetation beside or on the water.

Eggs: 5 to 8, chalky with green hue.

Food: Aquatic vegetation, will also graze on grasses.

Voice: Mainly hissing and grunting sounds.

Swans feature in many of our folklore tales, 'The Children of Lir' being one of the most popular stories.

Swans should be approached with caution, especially when breeding.

He made a swan-like end, fading in music.
Merchant of Venice: William Shakespeare

Kingfisher (Cruidín)

Kingfishers are shy secretive birds, found along slow-running rivers and streams. Often the only indication is the distinctive piercing single-noted call and then the flash of iridescent blue as they speed away in arrow-like flight. Their plumage is a dazzling blue/green colour with an orange/red underside. Their head is large with a long pointed bill. They have short wings and a short tail.

Kingfishers prefer to perch motionless on an overhanging branch watching the river for small fish. They will occasionally hover over water before darting down to plunge for fish. The male and female are similar, but the lower bill is black in the male and reddish/orange in the female. Kingfishers nest in deep burrows in a steep bank. Their food is mainly small fish and aquatic insects. During the winter months they tend to move nearer the coast.

Where: Rivers, canals and estuaries.
Nest: Long horizontal tunnel in river bank.
Eggs: 6 to 7, laid on bed of fish bones.
Food: Small fish, and aquatic invertebrates.

Kingfisher resting briefly after being ringed by Chris.

'KING OF FISHERS'

Kingfishers prefer slow-moving rivers where they can see the river bed.

Kestrel (Pocaire gaoithe)

Male 32cm / Female 36cm

The male is grey-blue on the head and nape, has a reddish back and wings with dark spots. The female is larger and is a chestnut colour with black barring. Kestrels are found in all kinds of habitat including cities and towns. This species has profited, to some degree, because of its association with man. They nest in hollow trees, church steeples, power stations and tall buildings in towns. Kestrels will readily use an artificial nestbox. They usually have one brood and the young fledge after thirty days. Immature kestrels are similar in colour to the female.

The kestrel is our commonest breeding falcon. It can be easily identified by the way it hovers over a piece of ground in search of small rodents and insects.

Where: Farmland, hillsides, sea cliffs, towns and cities.
Nests: On cliff faces, quarries, hollow trees and high buildings.
Eggs: Usually 3 to 6, whitish, with red/brown markings.
Food: Mainly small mammals and invertebrates.

Birds are highly visible and have few restricting boundaries (such as sea or land) so they are relatively easily studied in comparison to other fauna. Changes taking place in the world around us affect, not only us, but all sorts of wildlife. It is essential that we note these changes as it is often the effects on wildlife that are the first warning signals that something is going wrong. One of the key scientific tools that has been developed over the past 100 years for monitoring these changes is the marking and ringing of birds.

WHY RING BIRDS?

When you look at a blackbird in the garden, is it the same one that was there yesterday? How long has it been coming to the garden? Where was it last winter? Unless the blackbird has a particular distinguishing feature such as a white feather in the wing or a recognisable deformity, these questions will not be answered. Bird ringing came about as a result of these and many other questions that we, as humans, wanted to ask.

THE HISTORY of BIRD RINGING

The first historical record of bird ringing was as far back as the third century BC. Soldiers under seige from the Ligurians smuggled swallows out from the fortress to relieving troops. Messages were then attached to the birds' legs and the birds were released. The swallows flew back to the fortress, anxious to feed their young. The beseiged warriors were then able to read the messages and find out how long before help would arrive.

The earliest known scientific 'ringing' took place 775 years ago and was noted by the prior of a Cistercian monastery in Germany. He recorded that a man had taken an adult swallow from its nest and attached to its leg a piece of parchment

which said: 'Oh, Swallow, where do you live in winter?' The following spring the bird returned with an answer, 'In Asia, in the home of Petrus.'

During the eighteenth century J.L. Frisch, a German Ornithologist, disproved the then current theory that swallows spent the winter in the mud at the bottom of pools. He tied water-coloured dyed threads to their legs and when the birds appeared the following spring with the dye still visible he concluded that they had not hibernated under the water.

BIRD RINGING in IRELAND

What happens if you find a bird with a ring on? Well, the first thing you should do is send a letter to the address on the ring telling the person on what day you found the bird, where you found it, what the number is and, if you know it, the species of the bird.

Bird ringing in Ireland comes under the umbrella of the British Trust for Ornithology based in Norfolk, England. Bird ringers in Ireland are licensed by the National Parks and Wildlife Service. There are over 100 bird ringers in the 32 counties of Ireland. Each bird ringer has gone

Chris and Lorcan recording details of the ringed bird

through special training in the handling and identification of birds. The bird is ringed with its own uniquely numbered metal ring which makes it always recognisable as an individual. The safety and welfare of the bird is essential at all times.

Some of the most valuable information obtained by bird ringing is when the chicks are ringed in the nest. Not only is the age of the individual bird known but also exactly where the bird was born. One of the commonest methods used for capturing the birds is the Mist Net. This fine-meshed loose netting hangs from tightly drawn strings (shelf strings) that are attached to two vertical poles. The bird flies into the loose netting and falls down behind the stretched shelf string where it lies until collected by the bird ringer.

Lorcan Scott removing the bird from the mist net

Ringing the bird

Measuring the bird's wing

Other ways of catching birds include traps, some of which are quite sophisticated. Another and much rarer method of trapping birds is the Cannon Net. This is mainly used to catch waders and wildfowl. The net is camouflaged and when the birds are in the trapping area, the net is fired from a hidden place using small cannons. When the bird is caught it is identified and ringed and then a variety of other details is noted.

Do remember that if you ever come across nets or traps containing birds, do not interfere, but contact your local Garda, Wildlife Officer or Birdwatch Ireland.

Each of the Irish and British rings have the address: Natural History Museum, London SW7 and a unique number. Occasionally other types of ring or mark are attached to the bird so that it can be recognised from a distance. Large rings with two to five letter codes may be placed around the leg or neck in order that the bird can be individually identified without disturbing its normal activities. On smaller birds coloured rings can be attached in different ways so that they too can be identified from a distance. Some birds are fitted with wing or leg flags and

the dyeing of plumage is also carried out on certain groups from a particular area or of a particular age. In recent years more work is being done with the use of fitted radio and satellite transmitters. With the advent of technology and the computer chip becoming smaller every day even birds as small as blue tits are now being fitted with identifying chips that can be read from a discreet distance using a bar code receiver.

DETAILED INFORMATION

Particulars recorded include the ring number, species, age and weight of the bird. Other measurements, such as the wing length are also taken so that a guide to sub-species or even the sex of certain birds can be confirmed. Many other measurements can be taken and these depend on the particular scientific study being carried out.

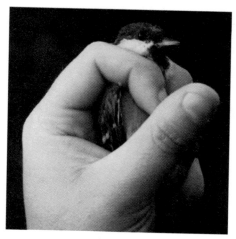

How to hold a small bird

Some Wildlife Group Descriptive Terms

BIRDS

Bevy of quails
Bevy of larks
Bevy of pheasants
Brace of dead game (2)
Brood of chickens
Cast of hawks
Charm of goldfinch
Clattering of chough
Colony of gulls
Covey of partridge
Covey of game birds
Dropping of shelduck
Exaltation of skylarks
Flight of birds
Flight of doves
Flight of swallows
Flock of birds
Flock of geese
Flock of wild duck
Gaggle of geese
Godliness of black-tailed godwit
Group of farm duck
Herd of cranes
Herd of swans
Herd of wrens
Little knot of wigeon
Murder of crows
Murmuration of starlings
Muster of peacocks
Nye of pheasants
Pack of grouse
Paddling of ducks
Parliament of owls
Raft of birds
Rookery of herons
Rookery of rooks

Rookery of penguins
Sedge of herons
Skein of ducks
Skein of geese
Spring of teal
Trip of wigeon
Ungodliness of bar-tailed godwit
Unkindness of ravens
Watch of nightingales
Wisp of snipe

NATURAL HISTORY

Array of hedgehogs
Catch of fish
Clump of trees
Colony of ants
Down of hares
Flight of bees
Haul of fish
Herd of seals
Hive of bees
Husk of hares
Nest of rabbits
Nest of ants
Pod of seals
Pod of whales
Rookery of seals
School of dolphins
School of whales
Shoal of mackerel
Shoal of fish
Shoal of herring
Skulk of foxes
Swarm of bees
Take of fish

Some Useful Wildlife Contact Addresses

An Taisce
The Tailor's Hall, Back Lane, Dublin 8
Telephone   01 - 4544794

Astronomy Ireland
PO Box 2888, Dublin1
Telephone   01 - 4598883

Burren National Park
2 Riverview, Corofin, Co. Clare
Telephone   065 - 37166

Connemara National Park
Letterfrack, Co. Galway
Telephone   095 - 41954

Earthwatch Friends of the Earth
Harbour View, Bantry, Co. Cork
Telephone   027 - 51283

ENFO
Andrew Street, Dublin 2
Telephone   01 - 6793144

Glenveagh National Park
Letterkenny, Co. Donegal
Telephone   074 - 37090

Geological Society of Ireland
c/o Dept. of Geography, UCD, Belfield, D. 4
Telephone   01 - 7068179

Irish Peatland Conservation Council
119 Capel Street, Dublin 1
Telephone   01 - 8722397

Irish Seal Sanctuary
Garristown, Co. Dublin
Telephone   01 - 8354370

ISPCA
300 Lower Rathmines Road, Dublin 6
Telephone   01 - 4977222

Irish Wildlife Trust
107 Lower Baggot Street, Dublin 2
Telephone   01 - 6768588

IWC Birdwatch Ireland
Ruttledge House, 8 Longford Place,
Monkstown, Co Dublin
Telephone   01 - 2804322

Killarney National Park
Muckross, Killarney, Co. Kerry
Telephone   064 - 31947

MET Éireann
Glasnevin Hill, Dublin 9
Telephone   01 - 8424411

National Parks and Wildlife Service
51 St. Stephen's Green, Dublin 2
Telephone   01 - 6613111

Voice
44 Upper Pembroke Street, Dublin 2
Telephone   01 - 6618123

Wexford Wildfowl Reserve
North Slob, Wexford
Telephone   053 - 23129

Wicklow Mountains National Park
Glendalough, Co. Wicklow
Telephone   0404 - 45338

Zoological Society of Ireland
Phoenix Park, Dublin 8
Telephone   01 - 6771425

British Trust for Ornithology
The Nunnery, Nunnery Place, Thetford,
Norfolk, IP24 2PU
Telephone   0044 - 1842 - 750050

Castle Espie, Wildfowl and Wetlands Trust Reserve
Ballydrain Road, Comber, Co. Down,
BT23 6EA
Telephone   (08) 01247 - 874146

Irish Naturalists' Journal
Ulster Museum, Botanic Gardens,
Belfast, BT9 5AB
Telephone   (08) 01232 - 383000

National Trust
86 Botanic Avenue, Belfast
Telephone   (08) 01232 - 230018

Royal Society for the Protection of Birds
The Lodge, Sandy, Bedfordshire, SG19 2DL
Telephone   0044 - 1767 - 680551

Books in the Series

Wildfile & Naturefile

Sparrowhawk (female)